KINGDOM LEADERSHIP

A CALL TO
CHRIST-CENTERED LEADERSHIP

MICHAEL D. MILLER

Convention Press
Nashville, Tennessee

5291-44
ISBN 0-8054-9295-X

Dewey Decimal Classification: 254.5
Subject Heading: CHURCH GROWTH\LEADERSHIP

Printed in the United States of America

All Scripture quotations are from the *New King James Version*.
Copyright © 1979, 1980, 1982, Thomas Nelson, Inc., Publishers.

The Sunday School Board of
the Southern Baptist Convention
127 Ninth Avenue North
Nashville, TN 37234

TABLE OF CONTENTS

FOREWORD

Occasionally, a book comes along that has the potential for helping ministers dramatically improve their lives and ministries. *Kingdom Leadership* is such a book. It contains biblical leadership principles that, if applied, will assure ministers a rich, fruitful, fulfilling life of Christian service. As I read this volume, I thought, *This is excellent. Every minister needs to read this book and, most of all, needs to live and practice its principles.*

Kingdom Leadership provides keen insight into the calling, character, competencies, and work of the kingdom leader. The book lifts up Jesus Christ as the ideal kingdom leader. It gives ministers a clear understanding of the kingdom leader's path. It enables them to identify the steps along this path and to move successively, naturally along the path, one step at a time.

Dr. Michael Miller has captured the essence and possibilities of being a God-called kingdom leader in a world that desperately needs such leaders. This volume points the way for every minister to be the kingdom leader God intends. It assures ministers who are in the smallest and hardest places and ministers who are in large, thriving churches that they all are a part of the bigger picture—the mighty, the glorious, the invincible kingdom of God.

The ideas, the hope, and the guiding principles in this volume have inspired and challenged me. They also will inspire and challenge you. *Kingdom Leadership* is destined to become a mainstay and guide for ministers who want to do God's will and fulfill His call in their lives and ministries.

James T. Draper, Jr.
President, Baptist Sunday School Board

INTRODUCTION

This book is about you and your calling to be a Christ-centered leader. This challenging call is life-changing, life-directing, and life-focusing. Once you have embarked on this Christ-centered leadership journey, your life will never be the same.

Why are many ministers trying to lead churches without following the model and having the power and guidance of the ideal Leader, Jesus Christ? Is it because they do not know Him and His leadership style? Have they chosen other leadership styles over the biblical model of kingdom leadership? Are they indifferent to the importance of the scriptural basis of church leadership? Each must answer for himself.

My purpose in this book is to portray Jesus Christ as the perfect model of biblical kingdom leadership and to urge every minister to adopt the Savior's leadership style as his own.

The power and influence of leaders are written on every page of human history. We have had leaders since the infancy of the race. And, we have had many different kinds of leaders. Some have brought civilization to the brink of destruction. Others have led the world through crises to triumph. The great need today is for Christ-centered leadership. The church desperately needs scriptural, spiritual leadership, rooted and grounded in the kingdom of God.

The better we understand the Bible, the more this truth becomes undeniably clear: *God calls leaders to lead His people in knowing and doing His will.* His call is more than merely a call to leadership. It is a call to *Christ-centered leadership.* The vital question is, How can we be Christ-centered leaders?

Church leaders are divided in their opinions about using secular business leadership principles in the church. Some feel that, because of the similarity between some business leadership principles and church leadership principles, church leaders can safely use these business principles. Other church leaders feel that using secular business principles removes the spiritual distinctions from the church's work and reduces it to just a business.

Churches reflect this debate in their structures and leadership styles. Some pastors view themselves as Chief Executive Officers (CEOs) rather than spiritual leaders. Their approach to church leadership is primarily business-oriented. Frequently, this approach causes confusion and frustration among church leaders and members.

The emphasis on church leaders using business leadership principles has resulted in most current Christian leadership discussions focusing on skills rather than on character. The problem is, many business models do not parallel the church's work. Business models focus on the functional aspects of leadership—leadership style, dealing with change, crisis management, relational skills, and other issues. Clearly, these issues are important for church leaders. But, to conclude that Christian leaders who have good business skills will be more effective in their work is false.

Business leadership models tend to focus on personality rather than on character. Many books on business leadership principles discuss in detail the personalities of significant business leaders. Rather than describing effective leaders' character traits, these materials often deal with effective leaders' personality traits. To describe Christian leadership and its effectiveness in terms of personality is risky. It suggests that leadership belongs only to those with certain personality traits.

Because of this overemphasis and dependency on secular business leadership principles, we urgently need to stress the importance of biblical principles as the foundation of Christ-centered

Should the church adopt secular business leadership principles?

Business models focus on skills and personality, not on character.

We urgently need to stress the importance of Christ-centered leadership.

leadership. This call to biblical principles is not a reaction to other leadership models. My purpose is to present the scriptural foundation of church leadership. This foundation is basic and essential for those who seek to be Christ-centered leaders.

The biblical truths we seek are inspired and were modeled by our Lord. Therefore, enter this study prayerfully and humbly.

You and I have been called and chosen to be kingdom leaders. Therefore, let us begin our journey with a sense of awe and an awareness of what God has in store for us.

Kingdom Leadership Begins with the Kingdom of God

The Bible is the foundation for all Christian leadership. To understand this foundation, let's begin with the kingdom of God.

The kingdom of God is a much neglected but mighty biblical truth. Many discussions of this grand doctrine either become mired in theological debate or relegate the kingdom to a place of unimportance in the work of the church.

The kingdom of God is the context within which the church is to comprehend and do its work. The kingdom gives church leaders an expanded vision and understanding of the magnitude of God's activity in the world. The kingdom gives confidence and assurance to the church and its leaders in every kind of situation.

The kingdom of God is the reign of God through Jesus Christ in the lives of persons as evidenced by God's activity in, through, and around them.

This graphic illustrates the universal nature of God's kingdom. It will appear in progressive stages of completion in the following chapters of this book. Its purpose is to help you visualize the various

My purpose is to present the scriptural foundation of church leadership.

The biblical truths we seek are inspired and were modeled by our Lord.

Leadership and the kingdom unite in Christ.

The kingdom of God is the context within which the church is to comprehend and do its work.

11

components of the fully equipped kingdom leader.

Jesus Christ and the Kingdom of God

Jesus is the King of the kingdom. Leadership and the kingdom unite in Him. The kingdom was the central focus of His ministry. The Gospels record over 100 instances where Jesus mentioned the kingdom. They record only two instances where He mentioned the church (Matt. 16:18; 18:17). That does not detract from the work of the church. It highlights the kingdom's importance.

Jesus' entire earthly ministry was set within the framework of the kingdom of God. He came preaching: *"The time is fulfilled, and the kingdom of God is at hand. Repent, and believe in the gospel"* (Mark 1:15). He told His disciples: *"It has been given to you to know the mysteries of the kingdom of heaven"* (Matt. 13:11). Throughout Jesus' earthly ministry, He preached and taught the kingdom's presence, power, and accessibility.

Christ gave the church six kingdom principles. These principles form a basic understanding of God's kingdom and its relationship to believers.

1. Jesus taught the kingdom of God is growing and cannot be stopped.

Jesus used parables about seeds sprouting, growing, and producing a harvest to illustrate the kingdom's growth. In Matthew 13:24–30, the good seeds of the kingdom grew and produced a harvest in spite of the weeds mixed in among them.

Jesus compared the kingdom to a mustard seed *"which indeed is the least of all the seeds; but when it is grown it is greater than the herbs and becomes a tree, so that the birds of the air come and nest in its branches"* (Matt. 13:32).

2. Jesus taught the kingdom of God is a reality, not simply a spiritual ideal.

Of course, the truths about the kingdom of God are mysterious to this world. That does not make

> Jesus' entire earthly ministry was set within the framework of the kingdom of God.

> God's kingdom is present and growing among us.

the kingdom any less real. Jesus gave His people, not the world, the privilege of knowing the revealed truths of God's kingdom (Matt. 13:11).

Scripture speaks of the kingdom as a reality. The kingdom can be seen (Mark 9:1; Luke 9:27; 19:11), entered into (Matt. 5:20; 21:31; John 3:5), and inherited (Matt. 25:43). Jesus is a real person. He expected to be joined by His disciples in the kingdom (Matt. 26:29).

The kingdom is from the heavenly world and possesses that world's realities and qualities (John 18:36), but it is no less real. In fact, that world is more real that ours.

3. Jesus taught that the kingdom of God is spiritual, not geographic.

Jesus declared, *"My kingdom is not of this world"* *(John 18:36)*. The kingdom of God is a spiritual reality. For believers, the kingdom begins in their hearts, is growing in the world, and will be completed in the end of the age by Christ Himself.

4. Jesus taught that the kingdom of God is community, not individuals.

God's kingdom is not a gathered group of individuals. It is a family. It involves interpersonal relationships with God and other believers. We are a kingdom of priests (1 Pet. 2:5; Rev. 1:6).

5. Jesus taught that the kingdom of God is universal, not local.

God's kingdom is eternal in its existence and universal in its scope. In the end of the age Jesus will send His angels throughout His kingdom to weed out all sin and evil (Matt. 13:41). That statement suggests the kingdom's vastness is beyond human comprehension.

6. Jesus taught that the kingdom of God is present among us and one day will be completed.

Christ said, *"the kingdom of heaven is at hand"*

The kingdom is a reality. It can be seen, entered into, and inherited.

For believers, the kingdom begins in their hearts, grows in their world, and is brought to full fruition in the end of the age by Christ Himself.

God's kingdom involves interpersonal relationships with God and other believers.

God's kingdom is eternal in its existence and universal in its scope.

God's kingdom is present with us and within us.

13

(Matt. 4:17). These words focus on the kingdom's presence in our world today. That presence is realized chiefly through God's reign in believers' hearts. Through His death and resurrection, Jesus opened the doors of the kingdom to humanity. Through the new birth believers enter the kingdom (John 3:3, 5).

Jesus promised that God's kingdom will be perfected in all of its glory and power. In Matthew 13:49 and elsewhere, Christ spoke of the end of the age as the time when the kingdom will be consummated. Paul declared in 1 Corinthians 15:24–25 that when Christ has destroyed all dominion, power, and authority—when He has put all His enemies under His feet—He will deliver up the consummated kingdom to God the Father.

> In the end of the age, God will perfect His kingdom in all of its glory and power.

God's kingdom focuses on the future. That future holds a glorious, perfected kingdom where God reigns in His fullness. No evil, no Satan, no death, no sorrow, and no suffering will invade that kingdom (Rev. 21:4). Only the power, presence, and peace of our glorious God will be there.

Daniel declared: *"And in the days of these kings the God of heaven will set up a kingdom which shall never be destroyed; and the kingdom shall not be left to other people; it shall break in pieces and consume all these kingdoms, and it shall stand forever"* (2:44).

> In the present, the Lord has called His church to carry out His purposes within the framework of His kingdom.

The church and its leaders can take heart and draw confidence from the kingdom of God. The kingdom is good news for a world impacted by injustice and evil. It's good news for churches who are struggling against the powers of darkness. It's good news for those who long to be free from the shackles of sin and lostness.

The central truth in Jesus' teachings is the presence, power, and accessibility of God's kingdom. This kingdom is growing. It cannot be stopped. The Lord has called His church to carry out His purposes within the framework of His kingdom. He calls, enables, and sends out His leaders to guide His church in extending His kingdom.

> God calls, enables, and sends out His leaders to guide His church in extending His kingdom.

14

1

Jesus Christ: The Kingdom Leader

Jesus Christ is the preeminent kingdom leader. His cross casts its shadow across the kingdom of God. It opens the kingdom to humanity and affirms Christ's unique role as the perfect model of the kingdom leader. Without Calvary, God's kingdom would have remained forever closed to the human race. Christ's sacrifice for our sins brings us salvation and sets before us the perfect model of kingdom leadership. Jesus embodies and exemplifies the essential principles of kingdom leadership that are indispensable for pastors and others called to lead local churches.

Even with Christ's pivotal work in establishing God's kingdom among us, Christian leaders often overlook Him as their primary leadership role model. They readily recognize Him as Lord and Savior but often pattern their ministries after prominent church leaders. Even so, it should be acknowledged that in His calling, character, and competencies, Jesus Christ is God's supreme example of kingdom leadership.

The apostle Paul challenged the church at Ephesus to measure its growth by *"the measure of the stature of the fullness of Christ" (Eph. 4:13).* Today's Christian leaders must accept the same challenge. Their leadership stands or falls when measured by God's standard—Jesus Christ.

Many church leaders are concerned about the future of Christian leadership. Some wonder whether effective leaders will be available to guide the church into the 21st century. Put your anxiety to rest! Don't worry! Look to Jesus, the leader of the church and the kingdom. He is the same yesterday, today, and forever (Heb. 13:8). Regardless of what happens today, tomorrow's church is secure in the hands of the perfect, eternal kingdom Leader. He will provide kingdom leaders for His churches.

Jesus' Titles Define His Person and Work

The Scriptures give Jesus many glorious titles. These titles represent His person, work, and leadership qualities. They describe who He is to the church and to believers and reflect the essential nature of kingdom leadership.

King of Kings

Jesus Christ is King of kings.—Revelation 19:16 declares that *"He has on His robe and on His thigh a name written: KING OF KINGS AND LORD OF LORDS."* The title "King of kings" affirms Jesus as supreme Ruler. He alone possesses ultimate power. He holds the right of absolute judgment. He stands above all government leaders and leaders of churches. He determines the future of kingdoms and earthly governments and directs His church in its work. Even under the most adverse circumstances, the church can rest assured that Jesus Christ is still the King of kings. During a time of intense persecution, the apostle John declared to the churches of Asia Minor that Jesus Christ is *"the faithful witness, the firstborn from the dead, and the ruler over the kings of the earth"* (Rev. 1:5).

Lord of Lords

Jesus Christ is Lord of lords (Rev. 19:16).—Christ is Lord and owner of all things. He is the church's absolute sovereign. The church belongs to Him.

Ultimate authority for all church functions and leadership resides in Him. Christ's lordship places all church leaders in the role of stewards. Until church leaders recognize Him as their sovereign Lord, they will never experience His lordship in their leadership of the church.

Captain of Salvation

Jesus Christ is the Captain of our salvation.—Hebrews 2:10 states that *"it became him, for whom are all things and by whom are all things, in bringing many sons unto glory, to make the captain of their salvation perfect through sufferings" (KJV).* As the church's Captain, Christ is always out front.

Through His suffering and death, Christ leads people into a new relationship with God. He embodies, exhibits, and surpasses supremely the sterling leadership qualities found among the world's greatest leaders. Christ's leadership, however, is kingdom leadership. He leads by love and devotion, not by might and coercion.

Christ is the frontline leader of His people. He alone can lead the way to God. He alone can empower and guide church leaders to lead God's people God's way to accomplish God's purposes. Church members and church leaders are to follow Him as His disciples.

Apostle

Jesus Christ is the Apostle.—Hebrews 3:1 proclaims: *"Therefore, holy brethren, partakers of the heavenly calling, consider the Apostle and High Priest of our confession, Christ Jesus."* An apostle is someone who has been commissioned to represent with authority the one who commissioned him. The title "Apostle" exalts Jesus Christ as the One who came from God the Father as His authoritative representative.

Jesus placed faithfulness at the heart of leadership. He was *"faithful to Him who appointed Him" (Heb. 3:2).* We have salvation and the church continues to grow because of Christ's faithfulness in His work on earth and His continued work in heaven. Like Christ, church leaders must anchor

Ultimate authority for all church functions and leadership resides in Christ.

Christ embodies, exhibits, and surpasses supremely the sterling leadership qualities found in earth's greatest leaders.

Christ alone can empower and guide church leaders to lead God's people God's way to accomplish God's purposes.

Jesus Christ came from God the Father as His authoritative representative .

17

their ministries in faithfulness to God, to their calling, to their families, and to their flocks.

High Priest
Jesus Christ is our great High Priest.—Hebrews 4:14 tells us that *"we have a great High Priest who has passed through the heavens, Jesus the Son of God, let us hold fast our confession."* Jesus Christ stands as the unique, supreme High Priest. He continues His priestly work on behalf of the church through His heavenly intercession (1 Tim. 2:5; 1 John 2:1). The priests of God in the Old Testament carried on God's work among His people, Israel. They served as leaders who represented the people to God. Christ alone is both the sacrifice and the presenter of the sacrifice before God.

Jesus made the church *"a holy priesthood, to offer up spiritual sacrifices acceptable to God through Jesus Christ" (1 Pet. 2:5).* Church leaders should not presume to be officiating "priests," but their ministries must embody the deep spiritual nature and functions that characterize Jesus' high priesthood.

Head of the Body
Jesus Christ is the Head of the body.—Colossians 1:18 exalts Jesus as *"the head of the body, the church, who is the beginning, the firstborn from the dead, that in all things He may have the preeminence."* Leadership and "headship" of the church are united in Christ. He alone has the right to determine what the church will be, where it will go, and what it will do. Church leaders hold their position as a trust from Him. They and the church are to function under His "headship" and in harmony with Him. Unless they do, the body can never function normally.

Chief Shepherd
Jesus Christ is the Chief Shepherd of the people of God (1 Pet. 5:4).—Jesus the Chief Shepherd nurtures, protects, and guides His churches. He chooses church leaders to carry out these functions as His

---

Church leaders must anchor their ministries in faithfulness to God, to their calling, to their families, and to their flocks.

Christ continues His priestly work on behalf of the church through His heavenly intercession.

Leadership and headship of the church are united in Christ.

undershepherds, but He forever remains the Chief Shepherd of the church.

What a beautiful picture of church leadership: Jesus Christ leading the church as a loving, caring shepherd through His undershepherds.

Overseer

Jesus Christ is the church's Overseer.—*"For you were like sheep going astray, but have now returned to the Shepherd and Overseer of your souls" (1 Pet. 2:25).* Jesus the Overseer watches over and directs His churches. He sees all of His churches and observes all that is going on in the lives of His people. He places the responsibilities of being overseers on church leaders, who are to follow His example.

Preeminent One

Jesus Christ is the Preeminent One.—Paul declared that *"in all things [Christ] may have the preeminence" (Col. 1:18).* Jesus Christ is to have first place in the lives of His people. He alone deserves the chief place in the church. He must have first place in church leaders' lives and calling. They must willingly, joyfully enthrone Him in His rightful position of preeminence in the church and in the lives of God's people with no thought of usurping His authority and glory.

Recognition of Jesus Christ as Leader of the church is fundamental to kingdom leadership. When the church grasps the mighty truth that Jesus is its preeminent Leader, great and exciting things begin to happen. His preeminence gives focus to the church's work and assures the church, especially in troubled times, that He will lead it to complete His (and its) work in the world.

When the church embraces Jesus as its preeminent Leader, God's power is released through the church. The gospel is declared, the kingdom of God is extended, and church leaders model true kingdom leadership.

Jesus' titles define the primary characteristics of

Christ chooses church leaders to nurture, protect, and guide the church as His undershepherds.

Jesus places the responsibilities of being overseers on church leaders, who are to follow His example.

The Lord alone deserves the chief place in the church and in church leaders' lives and calling.

Recognition of Jesus Christ as Leader of the church is fundamental to kingdom leadership.

19

kingdom leadership and help church leaders understand His leadership style—the only appropriate leadership style for church leaders.

Fundamental Kingdom Leadership Principles

Church leaders who submit to Jesus Christ as their **King** *recognize that their leadership appointment is an assignment from the King of kings.*—Christ's kingship and church leadership illustrate the kingdom principle of delegation. Jesus delegates His kingly authority to church leaders so His work can be carried out in the world.

Church leaders who acknowledge Jesus Christ as their **Lord** *learn the importance of stewardship.*—No church leader can claim the right of ownership. Christ owns all things. All leadership is a stewardship from Him. He gives leaders gifts and assigns places of service where each one may guide God's people to accomplish God's purposes.

Church leaders who follow Jesus Christ as their **Captain** *cannot hide from their kingdom responsibilities.*— Kingdom leadership requires sacrifice of self to the kingdom of God. Christian leaders must be next in line behind the Captain of salvation. They must position themselves in the forefront of their people in all spiritual battles. They cannot lag behind or take refuge in the rear guard, following their congregations rather than leading them.

Church leaders who embrace Jesus Christ as the **Apostle** *discover the importance of faithfulness.*— Faithfulness is essential for kingdom leadership. As the Apostle, Christ was faithful to the One who appointed Him. He set the example for all who would embody kingdom principles of leadership.

Church leaders who comprehend Christ's role as **High Priest** *realize kingdom leadership is spiritual.*— Kingdom leaders' fundamental call is a call to spiritual leadership. Jesus' high priestly ministry exemplifies the importance of this spiritual quality of kingdom leadership. His ministry teaches us that regardless of what else church leaders must

When the church embraces Jesus as its preeminent Leader, God's power is released through the church.

The only authority church leaders have is Christ's authority.

Leadership is a stewardship from Christ.

Kingdom leaders must position themselves in the forefront of their people in all spiritual battles.

20

do, nothing can displace their role as spiritual leaders.

Church leaders who grasp Christ's role as **Head of the body** *understand the critical importance of leadership coordination.*— As Head of the body, Christ determines the church's direction and expects its leaders and members to follow. Church leaders and the congregation are free to choose courses of action only within the framework of Christ's will for His church.

The church is to function as a body. It works as a whole. A body cannot be dissected and still be useful. Therefore, the kingdom principle of coordination between church leaders and congregation is of paramount importance.

What wondrous things, indeed, can be done when harmony within Christ's will prevails throughout the church.

Church leaders who recognize Christ as the **Chief Shepherd** *discover the principle of ministry leadership.*—Acts 20:28 and 1 Peter 5:2–4 describe the church as a flock and Jesus Christ as the Chief Shepherd. The Chief Shepherd guards, guides, and feeds the flock of God; and He calls His leaders to pattern their work after Him.

Church leaders who acknowledge Jesus Christ as **Overseer** *affirm the kingdom principle of oversight: a watchful and responsible care.*— As the Overseer of the church (1 Pet. 2:25), Christ embodies the oversight principle of leadership and shares the oversight of the church with its leaders (Phil. 1:1; 1 Tim. 3:2). They are to watch over the welfare, the work, and the fruit of the church and will give an account to God for their oversight. The Scriptures declare, *"for they watch out for your souls, as those who must give account"* (Heb. 13:17).

Church leaders who crown Jesus Christ as the **Preeminent One** *live out the principle of submission.*— Church leaders are never to seek first place. That position of honor and glory belongs to Jesus Christ alone. Church leaders are to have John the

Church leaders' fundamental call is a call to spiritual leadership.

The kingdom principle of coordination between Christ, church leaders, and congregation is of paramount importance.

Christ determines the church's direction and expects its leaders and members to follow.

Church leaders and the congregation are free to choose courses of actions only within the framework of Christ's will for His church.

21

Church leaders are
to watch over the
welfare, the work,
and the fruit of the
church and will give
an account to God
for their oversight.

Jesus Christ is
KING OF KINGS,
LORD OF LORDS,
Captain of salvation,
Apostle,
High Priest,
Head of the body,
Chief Shepherd,
Overseer,
Preeminent One.

Kingdom leadership
is:
sacrificial,
delegated,
stewardship,
faithfulness,
spiritual,
coordination,
ministry,
oversight,
submission.

Baptist's wholesome servant attitude: *"He must increase, but I must decrease" (John 3:30)*.

Kingdom Leadership Application

- Because Jesus is KING OF KINGS, kingdom leadership is *delegated.*
- Because Jesus Christ is LORD OF LORDS, kingdom leadership is *stewardship.*
- Because Jesus is Captain of salvation, kingdom leadership is *sacrificial.*
- Because Jesus Christ is Apostle, kingdom leadership is *faithfulness.*
- Because Jesus Christ is High Priest, kingdom leadership is *spiritual.*
- Because Jesus Christ is Head of the body, kingdom leadership is *coordination.*
- Because Jesus Christ is Chief Shepherd, kingdom leadership is *ministry.*
- Because Jesus Christ is Overseer, kingdom leadership is *oversight.*
- Because Jesus Christ is the Preeminent One, kingdom leadership is *submission.*

Jesus Christ is the incarnation of these fundamental kingdom leadership principles. Only as church leaders focus on Him as their model can they be assured of maximum leadership effectiveness.

Since these principles are so foundational to effective kingdom leadership, church leaders should develop and exhibit them constantly in their lives and ministries.

Kingdom Leadership Principle Number 1

- The kingdom of God sets the parameters for kingdom leaders.
- Jesus Christ is the essential kingdom leadership model.
- Kingdom leaders recognize and follow Christ as the preeminent leader of the church.

Kingdom Leadership Evaluation
Number 1

1. What leadership principles have you learned from Jesus' titles?
2. What are the implications for your leadership style when you consider Jesus as . . .
   A. KING OF KINGS?
   B. LORD OF LORDS?
   C. Captain of Salvation?
   D. Apostle?
   E. High Priest?
   F. Head of the body?
   G. Chief Shepherd?
   H. Overseer?
   I. Preeminent One?
3. Where do you feel God is directing you as the leader of your present church?
4. Where do you feel God is directing the church you currently serve?
5. List some ways you are following the Lord's leadership.
6. List some ways your church is following the Lord's leadership.
7. What steps are you taking to lead your church to follow the Lord?
8. Identify some areas in which you need to become a better follower of Christ.

KINGDOM LEADER APPLICATION

2

JESUS CHRIST: THE LEADER AND HIS CALLING

God's call to kingdom leadership is real. To comprehend that such a call actually happens is almost impossible. Yet it does, and it happens often. This call is even more astounding when we consider who does the calling—God Himself.

God's call is personal. Christ, the preeminent Leader of the church—the King of kings and Lord of lords—focuses His attention on individuals. He has a personal encounter with them and calls them to salvation and to service.

Who is worthy of such attention? Who is deserving? No one! Nevertheless, God in all His glory singles us out and calls us into kingdom service. (The kingdom leadership graphic now includes the cross and the call.)

God's call is a great mystery, far beyond our understanding. He approaches us, looks deep into our unworthy lives and says, "Come to Me. Come just as you are."

A miracle occurs when we overcome our unbelief and say, "Yes, Lord, I believe You died for me on the cross and rose again to give me eternal life. I ask You to forgive my sins and to take control of my life." In that moment, we experience the truth that *"as many as received Him, to them He gave the right to become children of God, even to those who believe in His name" (John 1:12).*

When this incredible event occurs, we enter the kingdom of God.

25

We are changed. The course of our lives is altered forever. We begin a lifelong journey of joy and service. Indeed, we begin a new life in which God's call will be affirmed again and again.

The Bible is filled with reassuring, instructive examples of God's call to salvation and to kingdom leadership.

"For you see your calling, brethren, that not many wise according to the flesh, not many mighty, not many noble, are called. But God has chosen the foolish things of the world to put to shame the wise, and God has chosen the weak things of the world to put to shame the things which are mighty...that no flesh should glory in His presence" (1 Cor. 1:26–27, 29).

God's call echoes throughout the Bible. Moses experienced that call. *"God called to him from the midst of the bush"* (Ex. 3:4), and *"[God] called to Moses out of the midst of the cloud"* (Ex. 24:16).

These great heroes of the faith—Abraham, Elijah, Elisha, Daniel, Amos, Jonah, Samuel, Matthew, John, Peter, and Paul—are but a few biblical examples among the hundreds whom God called into His service. Each person was unique, and each person was called of God.

Today, we who are called to kingdom service need to keep in mind that . . .

"We also, since we are surrounded by so great a cloud of witnesses, let us lay aside every weight, and the sin which so easily ensnares us, and let us run with endurance the race that is set before us, looking unto Jesus, the author and finisher of our faith, who for the joy that was set before Him endured the cross, despising the shame, and has sat down at the right hand of the throne of God" (Heb. 12:1–2).

God's call is essential and basic to Christian truth. Without it, no one would ever experience salvation. A world without the call of God would be a miserable, unbearable place. His call reveals that He is merciful and approachable, and it provides the church a model for evangelism.

God's call is indispensable for the Christian life.

First Peter 5:10 reminds us that *"the God of all grace, . . . called us to His eternal glory by Christ Jesus."* God's call to service is a profound experience. Unfortunately, that call seems largely to have been forgotten or is being disregarded today. Perhaps the reality of God's call is hard to accept, or the implications are too unsettling. In any case, believers cannot afford to lose touch with this pivotal truth.

Today's church must recover the freshness of God's presence. Peter says the church should tell *"the praises of Him who called you out of darkness into His marvelous light" (1 Pet. 2:9).*

A clear understanding of God's call enhances the church's success in carrying out the Great Commission.

God's call should be etched on our hearts and lives. It is the touchstone, the foundation for all that is to come in the life of a Christian. God's call secures leadership for His church and reassures believers in troubled times.

Defining God's Call

Just how should God's call be understood and defined? First, His call is an invitation to join Him in restored fellowship through receiving Jesus Christ as Savior and Lord. Then God's call is a summons to go with Him in His work of world redemption.

The call of God is solemn and serious business. The call comes from a holy God to a sinful world. Paul reminded young Timothy that God *"has saved us and called us with a holy calling . . . according to His own purpose and grace which was given to us in Christ Jesus before time began" (2 Tim. 1:9).* God calls us for His own purposes and glory. His call to salvation is a call of grace to every person, regardless of who they are.

God's call is an invitation to enter the kingdom of God. Paul encouraged the Thessalonians to *"walk worthy of God who calls you into His own kingdom and glory" (1 Thess. 2:12).* What a marvelous

---

A clear understanding of God's call enhances the church's success in carrying out the Great Commission.

God's call is the touchstone, the foundation for all that is to come in the life of a Christian.

God's call to salvation is a call of grace to every person, regardless of who they are.

truth! God calls sinful people to Himself and to salvation through Jesus Christ. No greater honor or privilege comes to a person than to be invited to enter the kingdom of God.

God Calls Us to Join Him
Called to Salvation

Jesus invites persons to enter a new relationship with God. The "Call of God" graphic illustrates His invitation and people's response. Christ proclaimed: *"Come to Me, all you who labor and are heavy laden, and I will give you rest"* (Matt. 11:28).

Jesus' invitation is a call to eternal life. It is an invitation to experience peace with God that comes only through receiving Jesus Christ as Savior and Lord. This is the greatest invitation ever offered to anyone. Paul told Timothy to *"lay hold on eternal life, to which you were also called"* (1 Tim. 6:12).

God

Call of God

Come and
join me

Called to Be Holy

The New Testament expands the truth of God's call. Christians not only are called to a new relationship with Christ, they also are called to a life of holiness (1 Thess. 4:7). Paul declared that we are *"called to be saints"* (Rom. 1:7; 1 Cor. 1:2). We are called to be separated from sin and to be set apart for God's service. The New Testament term for this experience and process is *sanctification.*

Called to Security

God does not rescind His call to salvation. Speaking of God's call of Israel to redemption, Paul declared that *"the gifts and the calling of God are irrevocable"* (Rom. 11:29).

God's call to salvation keeps believers secure. It anchors their salvation and comforts their hearts in the ⁀rms of life. For *"whom He called, these He also justified; and whom He justified, these He also glorified"* (Rom. 8:30).

God's call is neither random nor arbitrary. He

calls us *"according to His purpose" (Rom. 8:28),* and His call keeps the church and believers secure.

God Calls Us to Go with Him
Called to Serve

God calls believers to service. Perhaps the classic passage of Scripture concerning God's call to service is Isaiah 6:1–8. After Isaiah saw the Lord in His majesty and glory, the prophet declared: *"Also I heard the voice of the Lord, saying: 'Whom shall I send, And who will go for Us?' Then I said, 'Here am I! Send me' " (Isa. 6:8).* Like Isaiah, the church's response to God's call must be, "Here am I! Send me!"

The "Call of God" graphic now illustrates that God's call to service is a call to go with Him in His work in the world. He does not call us to serve alone. We are to accompany *Him* on *His* mission. Did not Jesus promise, *"Lo, I am with you always, even to the end of the age" (Matt. 28:20)?*

The Lord first invites us to come to Him. Then He calls us to *"go therefore and make disciples of all the nations, baptizing them in the name of the Father and of the Son and of the Holy Spirit, teaching them to observe all things that I have commanded you" (Matt. 28:19–20).*

God's call is the church's commission from Jesus Christ. It is a mandate to carry out the Great Commission. And, the church is to respond affirmatively to its call to serve the Lord.

Called to Suffer

God calls us to suffer if need be in carrying out the Great Commission. Peter wrote, *"For to this you were called, because Christ also suffered for us, leaving us an example, that you should follow His steps" (1 Pet. 2:21).*

Suffering and sacrifice in God's service are not popular among Christians today. But the fact is, God's call is a call to self-denial and suffering. Jesus made it clear that *"if anyone desires to come after*

God's call keeps the church and believers secure.

God does not call us to serve alone. We are to accompany *Him* on *His* mission.

God's call to the church is its mandate to carry out the Great Commission.

God

Call of God

Come and join me

Go with me

29

Me, let him deny himself, and take up his cross, and follow Me" (Matt. 16:24). Answering God's call to follow Christ means denying ourselves and being willing to suffer for His sake.

God's call is a call to self-denial and suffering.

Answering God's call assures a measure of suffering. But with the pressure of suffering comes the promise of God's presence and provision. Those who hear His call to service also hear His promises and find comfort in them.

"No temptation has overtaken you except such as is common to man; but God is faithful, who will not allow you to be tempted beyond what you are able, but with the temptation will also make the way of escape, that you may be able to bear it" (1 Cor. 10:13).

Understanding God's call is essential to being a kingdom leader. God calls us to join Him in fellowship and to go with Him in service, knowing that His call to service includes a call to suffering.

God calls us to join Him in fellowship and to go with Him in service.

Jesus Christ:
The Leader and the Call of God

No one better illustrates the reality of God's call than Jesus Himself. His life perfectly models unconditional response to God's call.

Christ teaches us the importance of faithfulness to God's call. Hebrews 3:1 calls Him the *Apostle*— One sent on a mission with the authority of the One who commissioned Him. Hebrews 3:2 declares He *"was faithful to Him who appointed Him."*

Jesus enjoys eternal fellowship with the Father. Christ prayed: *"And now, O Father, glorify Me together with Yourself, with the glory which I had with You before the world was" (John 17:5).* Again, He declared: *"As You, Father, are in Me, and I in You" (John 17:21)* and *"the Father is in Me, and I in Him" (John 10:38).*

Jesus' life perfectly models unconditional response to God's call.

Jesus Christ and His Response
to God's Call

Jesus did not need to be invited into fellowship with the Father, but He did receive a call to service. God's call authorized and empowered Christ to accomplish God's purposes in the world. Jesus said concerning His call, *"My food is to do the will of Him who sent Me, and to finish His work" (John 4:34)*.

Ways Jesus Responded to God's Call

First, Christ said only what God the Father said.— Jesus proclaimed: *"For I have not spoken on my own authority; but the Father who sent Me gave Me a command, what I should say and what I should speak. . . . Therefore, whatever I speak, just as the Father has told Me, so I speak" (John 12:49–50)*. Kingdom leaders are to follow Christ's example. They are to say what God wants them to say—no more, no less.

*Second, Jesus did only the works the Father gave Him to do.—*Jesus said, *"the works which the Father has given Me to finish—the very works that I do—bear witness of Me, that the Father has sent Me" (John 5:36)*.

Jesus' every action and word focused on accomplishing the Father's will. Christ's call and commission were constantly on His mind throughout His earthly ministry. He spoke repeatedly of God sending Him—24 times in the Gospel of John alone.

All kingdom leadership is driven and guided by God's call to join Him in His work in the world.

Third, Jesus went only where the Father sent Him.— Jesus did not act independently of the Father. He always acted on the Father's directions and lived in total submission to His will. The Savior said, *"I have come down from heaven, not to do My own will, but the will of Him who sent Me" (John 6:38)*.

Jesus' passion and single-minded purpose was to accomplish the work God had given Him to do. In the garden of Gethsemane, just hours before His crucifixion, Jesus cried, *"Not My will, but Yours be done" (Luke 22:42)*.

Like Jesus, kingdom leaders rejoice to do God's will. They are constantly aware of being commissioned by the Lord to go and make disciples.

Jesus Christ and His Call to the Church

Jesus commissioned His disciples to carry out His

> Kingdom leaders are to say what God wants them to say— no more, no less.

> All kingdom leadership is driven and guided by God's call to join Him in His work in the world.

> Jesus' passion and single-minded purpose was to accomplish the work God had given Him to do.

purpose in the world. He prayed to His Father, *"As You sent Me into the world, I also have sent them into the world" (John 17:18).*

The Lord's call to the church is clear: *"Go therefore and make disciples of all the nations, baptizing them in the name of the Father and of the Son and of the Holy Spirit, teaching them to observe all things that I have commanded you; and lo, I am with you always, even to the end of the age" (Matt. 28:19–20).*

Christ made the church's task clear. That task is to carry out the Great Commission. The church evangelizes, disciples, ministers, fellowships, and worships—the five basic church functions—as it fulfills God's call. To deviate from that purpose is to reject God's will and the church's calling.

Jesus Christ and the Gift of Leadership
The Gift of Leaders

God provides Christ-centered leaders for the church. These leaders are to guide the church in carrying out His will. The kingdom leader has a special call to leadership. Kingdom leadership is initiated by the call of God. Paul expressed this sentiment for all who are called to leadership when he said, *"I thank Christ Jesus our Lord who has enabled me, because He considered me faithful, putting me into the ministry"(1 Tim. 1:12).*

Ephesians. 4:11–13 states: *"And He Himself gave some to be apostles, some prophets, some evangelists, and some pastors and teachers, for the equipping of the saints for the work of ministry, for the edifying of the body of Christ, till we all come to the unity of the faith and the knowledge of the Son of God, to a perfect man."*

Kingdom leaders are God's gift to the church. The Ephesians passage says, *"He Himself gave."* The Lord personally selects and presents leaders to the church. These leaders have various functions. Some are apostles, some prophets, some evangelists, and some pastors and teachers. Regardless of leaders' functions, the church should recognize them as a gift from the Lord.

Kingdom leaders rejoice to do the will of God.

The church evangelizes, disciples, ministers, fellowships, and worships as it fulfills God's call.

Kingdom leaders are God's gift to the church.

The Leadership Guarantee

A current misconception suggests that all effective church leaders are passing from the scene. Fear grips the hearts of church members who wonder how these effective leaders will be replaced. The answer is: The Lord will replace them. He will not leave His church without kingdom leaders. He guarantees His church leadership until it has completed its calling and purpose. Christ will provide His church leaders until *"we all come to the unity of the faith"* (Eph. 4:13).

God guarantees His church leadership until it has completed its calling and purpose.

The Stewardship for Leaders

Paul's statement to the Ephesian church suggests that every church has a stewardship responsibility for its leaders. When God gives a gift, a stewardship responsibility goes with it. Therefore, churches have God-given responsibilities to the leaders God has given them.

Churches must be good stewards of God's gifts. Along with personal spiritual gifts to do the work of ministry, God has gifted churches with leaders. Churches are to care for, minister to, strengthen, and support the leaders God has entrusted to them. Paul's counselled the church: *"Let the elders who rule well be counted worthy of double honor, especially those who labor in the word and doctrine. . . . The laborer is worthy of his wages"* (1 Tim. 5:17–18).

Churches have God-given responsibilities to the leaders God has given them.

The Stewardship of Leaders

Kingdom leaders are stewards of the leadership gifts and roles God has given them. These leaders understand that they were selected by the Lord to follow Him and to guide the church in accomplishing the Great Commission. Paul said, *"Let a man so consider us, as servants of Christ and stewards of the mysteries of God"* (1 Cor. 4:1).

Just as churches are stewards of their leaders, leaders are stewards of their churches. This stewardship is a mutual responsibility. It is an awesome but joyous responsibility for churches and leaders.

Just as churches are stewards of their leaders, leaders are stewards of their churches.

33

Jesus was faithful to the One who appointed Him. Kingdom leaders likewise must recognize the importance of being faithful to God's appointment as leaders in the churches.

The Call of God and the Kingdom Leader's Life

Kingdom leadership focuses on Jesus Christ. He represents the essence of leadership. His life defines and models leadership in word and deed.

God calls kingdom leaders to equip and build up churches.—Their chief work is to lead churches to carry out the Great Commission.

God calls kingdom leaders to deliver His message to the churches.—Jesus modeled this principle perfectly. He spoke only what the Father instructed Him to speak. Old Testament prophets declared, "Thus saith the Lord." Therefore, kingdom leaders are to remain faithful to the message the Lord gives them to deliver.

Unfortunately, leaders sometimes may spend time speaking about issues that are not appropriate, timely, or relevant to the churches' needs. Kingdom leaders must evaluate their speech by what God wants to say to the churches, and their speech must agree with God's message.

God calls kingdom leaders to do only the work He gives them to do.—Jesus perfectly modeled this principle. He came to do the works of God and did them with directness and clear purpose.

Church leaders are busier than ever. Busyness, however, does not always mean doing the Lord's work. Leaders must know what God wants them to do and devote their time and energy to doing it.

God calls the church to do the works Christ gave it to do.—Jesus did the works the Father gave Him to do, and He promises churches power to do whatever He directs them to do. He said, *"He who believes in Me, the works that I do he will do also; and greater works than these he will do, because I go to My Father"* (John 14:12).

Kingdom leaders' chief work is to lead churches to carry out the Great Commission.

Kingdom leaders are to remain faithful to the message the Lord wants them to deliver to the churches.

Kingdom leaders must know what God wants them to do and concentrate their time and energy on doing it.

Kingdom leaders serve willingly in the place of service the Lord assigns them.—Jesus was never anxious about where the Father sent Him. He faithfully completed the work of redemption. He fulfilled His calling even to death. Kingdom leaders are to be content and happy in the place to which God has assigned them.

The Lord chooses where His leaders serve. This divine guidance reassures leaders as they seek to discover where God wants them to serve. When this principle is understood, leaders need not be jealous of other leaders and their assigned places of service. For God directs all His leaders according to His plan to their particular places of service.

Obedience is essential for kingdom leaders.—Nothing better describes Christ's response to the Father's call than *obedience*. Paul declared, *"He . . . became obedient to the point of death" (Phil. 2:8).*

When the Lord sends a leader to a place of service, He gives the leader specific work to do. The kingdom leader makes it his life goal to obey the Lord and to complete the work.

Kingdom leaders live in full assurance God will gift them to accomplish their leadership roles in the church.—God selects His leaders and gives them ministry gifts to accomplish His purposes.

When Peter and John were arrested for their ministry in Jerusalem, they preached with authority before the same rulers who had crucified Christ. God gave the two disciples their courage and frankness. The rulers' response to Peter's sermon underscores this truth: *"Now when they saw the boldness of Peter and John, and perceived that they were uneducated and untrained men, they marveled. And they realized that they had been with Jesus" (Acts 4:13).*

Peter and John lacked formal training and skills, but God called and gifted them to be strong witnesses for Him. God never calls a person to leadership without gifting that person for that specific task.

> God directs all His leaders according to His plan to their particular places of service.

> Kingdom leaders are to be content and happy in the place to which God has called them.

Kingdom Leadership Principle
Number 2

- God's call is the foundation of the church's work in the world.
- Kingdom leaders are a gift from God to equip churches to accomplish their calling from God.
- Kingdom leaders must first follow God's call to be disciples. Then they must be sensitive to His call to leadership.

Kingdom Leadership Evaluation
Number 2

1. Write an account of your call to salvation and to leadership.
2. In what ways do members of your church understand their stewardship for the leaders Christ has entrusted to them?
3. In what ways are you as a kingdom leader guiding the church to focus on the Great Commission as the primary purpose of the church?
4. How can you as a kingdom leader help the church understand and practice biblical stewardship for its leaders?
5. Write a description of your stewardship of the leadership the Lord has given you as a kingdom leader.
6. What improvements do you need to make in your response to your call to be a kingdom leader?

Jesus Christ:
The Leader and His Character

"Therefore God also has highly exalted Him and given Him the name which is above every name, that at the name of Jesus every knee should bow, of those in heaven, and of those on earth, and of those under the earth, and that every tongue should confess that Jesus Christ is Lord, to the glory of God the Father" (Phil. 2: 9–11).

Where shall we look for our model for the kingdom leader's character? To the Lord Jesus Christ, of course! His character has no rival and no peer. His character is flawless; His integrity is impeccable. Wherever Jesus was—whether in a crowd, at a feast, teaching on a hillside, confronting evil adversaries, resisting opponents, or facing temptations— His words and actions clearly revealed that His character was faultless, authentic, and consistent.

Kingdom leaders must embrace Jesus' character as their ideal. He built His leadership on the solid foundation of His character, character that was tested and proved in the fires of real life encounters. Jesus obeyed God's call without hesitation. He faced every difficulty without failure. And, He did it as an authentic human being. Therefore, He is our model and example of kingdom leadership.

A Balanced Life
Where shall we look for an example of the kingdom leader's balanced

life? Again, we look to Jesus. His personal development illustrates the leader lifestyle we seek.

Jesus' life was characterized by balanced growth and development. He grew spiritually, physically, emotionally, and socially. Luke declares, *"And the Child grew and became strong in spirit, filled with wisdom; and the grace of God was upon Him"* (2:40).

Even though Jesus was the divine Son of God, Luke assures us that He learned and developed like any other person: *"And Jesus increased in wisdom and stature, and in favor with God and men"* (2:52). Therefore, it is not too much to suggest that Christ's character revealed itself as He grew from childhood into adulthood.

An incident occurred in Jesus' life when He was 12 years old that underscores the balance in His life. Jesus had gone with Mary and Joseph to Jerusalem for the Feast of the Passover. While there, Jesus went alone to the temple. Mary and Joseph searched for Him and found Him sitting among the teachers, listening and asking questions. All who heard Him were astonished at His understanding and answers.

Although Jesus was the Son of God and had such wisdom at such an early age, He also obeyed Mary and Joseph and returned to Nazareth with them.

Jesus' balanced personal growth set the pattern for all kingdom leaders. Indeed, no person can be a true kingdom leader without the foundation of a balanced life modeled after Jesus Christ.

Personal Holiness

The trials Jesus endured confirmed His character. Even in the face of a hostile, sinful world, He remained free from sin. Such unblemished conduct could only come from flawless character.

Hebrews proclaims that Christ *"is holy, harmless, undefiled, separate from sinners, and has become higher than the heavens"* (7:26).

The pressures kingdom leaders endure forge their character. God calls leaders to carry out the

---

Jesus' personal development illustrates the leader lifestyle we seek.

Christ's character revealed itself as He grew from childhood into adulthood.

Jesus' personal growth set the pattern for all kingdom leaders.

Christ's unblemished conduct could only come from flawless character.

Great Commission and sends them into a hostile world. When pressures rise against them and the gospel, leaders' character is tested and matured.

Resistance to Sin

Jesus was the divine Son of God. Nevertheless, He experienced the pressure of temptation (Matt. 4:1–11). The Scripture assures us that *"we do not have a High Priest who cannot sympathize with our weaknesses, but was in all points tempted as we are, yet without sin" (Heb. 4:15).*

Jesus experienced the strain and pressure of temptation all kingdom leaders endure. He overcame temptation and enables us to have victory over sin. Hebrews declares: *"For in that He Himself has suffered, being tempted, He is able to aid those who are tempted" (2:18).*

Faithfulness

Jesus *"was faithful to Him who appointed Him" (Heb. 3:2).* Christ demonstrated that faithfulness by carrying out God's will regardless of the consequences. Such faithfulness is absolutely essential for all kingdom leaders.

Obedience

Jesus' life was not without pain. In fact, the Lord suffered more intensely than any person who ever lived.

"In the days of His flesh, when He had offered up prayers and supplications, with vehement cries and tears to Him who was able to save Him from death, and was heard because of His godly fear, though He was a Son, yet He learned obedience by the things which He suffered. And having been perfected, He became the author of eternal salvation to all who obey Him" (Heb. 5:7–9).

Jesus' character was shaped and molded by His suffering. *"He learned obedience by the things which He suffered."*

Kingdom leaders soon learn that faithful obedience to God brings suffering. But, such suffering is the crucible in which their character is refined and they are prepared for kingdom service.

The pressures kingdom leaders endure forge their character.

Jesus experienced the strain and pressure of temptation all kingdom leaders endure.

Faithfulness is absolutely essential for all kingdom leaders.

Jesus' character was shaped and molded by His suffering.

Self-Sacrifice

Of all the terms that best describe Jesus' character, *self-sacrificing* is the superlative one. Christ, the Lord of glory, put aside all the comforts of heaven, all His privileges, all His splendor to come and give His life for the sins of the world. Paul wrote that Jesus *"made Himself of no reputation, taking the form of a servant" (Phil. 2:7).*

Jesus sacrificed His all in order to do the work of God the Father. Such self-sacrifice clearly demonstrates His unsurpassed, God-given character and establishes God's pattern for all kingdom leaders.

Humility

Jesus embodied humility, an essential characteristic of all kingdom leaders. *"He humbled Himself and became obedient to the point of death, even the death of the cross" (Phil. 2:8).*

Christ spent His life in the midst of a sinful world, yet He was holy and sinless. He experienced temptations but did not sin. He was the perfect Son of God; still He learned obedience from what He suffered. He humbled Himself. He sacrificed glory, honor, and authority to fulfill His God-given mission.

Jesus embodied and displayed the kind of character that is essential for all church leaders. Church leaders will discover and develop the character required for kingdom leadership only when they embrace Christ as their role model.

Christian Character Development

Character and integrity are the bedrocks of Christian ministry. Both are essential for kingdom leaders. Without integrity, churches and church leaders shed no light in a sin-darkened world.

The Path of Character Formation

As long as Christians remain in this world, God is going to develop their character. Paul said, *"We also glory in tribulations, knowing that tribulation produces perseverance; and perseverance, character; and character, hope" (Rom. 5:3–4).*

These verses describe the path of character development for Christians. That path leads through trials. Trials come because of the church's and believers' commitment to obey God's call. But remember, trials produce endurance. Endurance produces character. Character is tested integrity, and endurance is needed to do God's will. While character is developing, hope is experienced.

Some people think Christians are exempt from suffering, trials, and adversity. Jesus' life reveals that is a mistaken idea. *"All who desire to live godly in Christ will suffer persecution" (2 Tim: 3:12).* Troubles often increase for Christians who live according to kingdom principles. In fact, kingdom leadership often places church leaders under stresses other Christians never experience.

Trials Christians endure result in identification with Christ. He warned us that *"if the world hates you, you know that it hated Me before it hated you" (John 15:18).*

Christians should not expect better treatment than Jesus received. *"A disciple is not above his teacher, nor a servant above his master. It is enough for a disciple that he be like his teacher, and a servant like his master" (Matt. 10:24–25).*

In spite of the world's hate, Jesus demonstrated hope-filled character. He expects His church and it's leaders to have the same hope-filled character.

Character and the Kingdom Leader

Perhaps no section of Scripture has been overlooked more in relationship to kingdom leaders' character than Paul's Pastoral Letters. These letters provide leaders a wealth of help in understanding the kind of character God expects in His leaders.

The Pastoral Letters focus on leaders' character, not on skills. Too many church leaders mistakenly have spent all or most of their time developing preaching, administrative, and ministry skills without giving equal or greater attention to character building. These skills are important, but character is far more important.

The path of character development for Christians leads through trials.

Troubles often increase for Christians who live according to kingdom principles.

Christians should not expect better treatment than Jesus received.

41

The kingdom leader is a person of Christlike character. In the Pastoral Letters, Paul used the word *godliness* to describe the kingdom leader's character. The apostle said to Timothy, *"exercise yourself rather to godliness" (1 Tim. 4:7).*

Every church leader is to develop spiritual disciplines to meet the demands of kingdom leadership. Every leader is to lead a disciplined, godly life.

Kingdom leaders must pay particular attention to personal holiness. Paul challenged Timothy to *"take heed to yourself and to the doctrine. Continue in them, for in doing this you will save both yourself and those who hear you" (1 Tim. 4:16).*

The promise is that leaders who model their lives after Jesus Christ will save themselves and those who hear them. The greatest gifts a kingdom leader can give to His church are personal integrity and holiness.

As Christ exemplified God's standard of character, a kingdom leader must exemplify Christlike character before all people, especially the church. Leaders are to *"be an example to the believers in word, in conduct, in love, in spirit, in faith, in purity" (1 Tim. 4:12).* Church leaders are to set the pattern for how believers should talk, live, demonstrate love, grow spiritually, trust the Lord, and live godly lives. What a challenge for kingdom leaders!

Kingdom leaders show their Christlike character by living contented lives. Contentment is the ability to be at peace with yourself regardless of the circumstances. Paul declared, *"Godliness with contentment is great gain. For we brought nothing into this world, and it is certain we can carry nothing out." (1 Tim. 6:6–7).* Scriptural contentment adds effectiveness to kingdom leaders' work.

Kingdom leaders must keep watch over their hearts and minds to avoid becoming discontented. The kingdom leader who is not contented can fall to the temptations of materialism. Paul described the dangers of these temptations: *"And having food and clothing, with these we shall be content.*

But those who desire to be rich fall into temptation and a snare, and into many foolish and harmful lusts which drown men in destruction and perdition" (1 Tim. 6: 8–9). The apostle warned Timothy to preach these truths and to live by them.

Many church leaders have been destroyed by lack of contentment in ministry. Paul reminded Timothy to flee the entrapments of materialism and to pursue Christlike character: *"But you, O man of God, flee these things and pursue righteousness, godliness, faith, love, patience, gentleness. Fight the good fight of faith, lay hold on eternal life, to which you were also called" (1 Tim. 6:11–12).*

Righteousness, godliness, faith, love, patience, and gentleness are the essential character qualities kingdom leaders should cultivate constantly. These qualities are rooted in the person and character of Jesus Christ.

Character and Leadership Selection in the Church

Each church is responsible for choosing its leaders according to biblical standards. Many churches, however, do not take this task seriously enough.

Qualifications for church leaders center on character, not on skills. Churches that are searching for those who have been chosen by God as kingdom leaders would do well to know and understand what character qualities God expects in these leaders. Paul leaves no uncertainty about that issue. He described these essential qualities in 1 Timothy 3:1–7. Regardless of a person's ministerial role, these qualities represent God's standard for kingdom leaders.

Desire to Serve
Kingdom leaders are to have a passion to serve and to lead.—Paul said, *"If a man desires the position of a bishop, he desires a good work" (1 Tim. 3:1).* This desire is not selfish ambition. It is a genuine conviction that God has called that person to leadership in that church.

Scriptural contentment adds effectiveness to kingdom leaders' work.

Righteousness, godliness, faith, love, patience, and gentleness are the essential character qualities kingdom leaders should cultivate constantly.

Qualifications for church leaders center on character, not on skills.

43

Those who lead the church should do so because they have a God-given aspiration to serve. If a person has no desire to lead the church, that person will not be an effective leader of the church.

Blameless

Kingdom leaders are to be blameless.—Paul declared, *"A bishop then must be blameless" (1 Tim. 3: 2).* Kingdom leaders are not to have hidden personal agendas. Their character and lives are to be above reproach. They are to live so well that people cannot bring legitimate charges against them.

Husband of One Wife

Kingdom leaders are to be faithful to their wives.— First Timothy 3:2 states, *"A bishop then must be . . . the husband of one wife."* This is God's standard for marriage. It impresses the church with the importance of faithfulness in marriage and establishes the kingdom leader as a model of marital commitment.

Temperate

Kingdom leaders are to be self-controlled.—Paul affirmed that *"a bishop then must be . . . temperate" (1 Tim. 3:2).* Church leaders are to exhibit temperance and restraint in all areas of life. They are to demonstrate physical, spiritual, emotional, and social balance in their lives. Kingdom leaders are to exercise self-control in mind, body, and spirit.

Sober-minded and of Good Behavior

Kingdom leaders are to be sensible and serious.— "A bishop then must be . . . sober-minded, of good behavior" (1 Tim. 3:2). Kingdom leaders are to be mentally and emotionally stable. They are not to be biased in their judgment. Rather, they are to be prudent and discerning.

Kingdom leaders are to conduct their lives with dignity and orderliness.—Their lives are to reveal an inner stability. When others observe these leaders, they need to see behavior worthy of emulation.

Those who lead the church should do so because they have a God-given aspiration to serve.

Church leaders' character and lives are to be above reproach.

Kingdom leaders are to exercise self-control in mind, body, and spirit.

Hospitable

Kingdom leaders are to exhibit hospitality.— "*A bishop then must be . . . hospitable*" *(1 Tim. 3:2).* Church leaders are not to provide just for their family or friends. They are to show hospitality and politeness to outsiders and strangers. The church must always be open to strangers, and church leaders are to model this quality for the congregation.

Able to Teach

Kingdom leaders are to be capable and qualified to teach the truths of the Christian faith.— "*A bishop then must be . . . able to teach*" *(1 Tim. 3: 2).* Teaching is an exceptionally valuable gift. To be able to rightly divide the word of truth and to help people know and practice God's Word are precious gifts.

Not Given to Wine

Kingdom leaders are not to be involved in alcohol abuse.— "*A bishop then must be . . . not given to wine*" *(1 Tim. 3: 2–3).* Kingdom leaders are not to fall under the control of alcohol or other drugs. The Greek word Paul used for "not given" suggests the idea of freedom from dependency on any type of addicting substance.

Not Violent, but Gentle

Kingdom leaders are not to indulge in violent behavior.— "*A bishop then must be . . . not violent, . . . but gentle, not quarrelsome*" *(1 Tim. 3:2–3).* Church leaders do not settle disputes with blows—either physically or verbally. They are not quick-tempered. They do not browbeat people in order to win their case. Kingdom leaders are flexible and approachable. They yield when they are wrong. They do not manipulate others. Rather they embrace Jesus as their model of gentleness.

Not Argumentative

Kingdom leaders are not to be argumentative.—The word *quarrelsome* indicates a verbal fighter. Christlike leaders do not verbally attack others.

Kingdom leaders' lives are to reveal an inner stability.

Church leaders are to show hospitality and politeness to outsiders and strangers.

To be able to help people know and practice God's Word is a precious gift.

Church leaders are not to fall under the control of alcohol or other drugs.

45

Neither do they spend their time in useless debates and wars of words.

Not Greedy for Money nor Covetous

Kingdom leaders' lives are not to focus on material things.—"A bishop then must be . . . not greedy for money" (1 Tim. 3:2–3). God's leaders do not place an overemphasis on wealth. Neither do they desire things that belong to others. Kingdom leaders are content with income adequate to meet their needs and to carry on their ministry. They focus their lives and energies on the work of God's kingdom. Kingdom leadership requires sharing and giving, not a covetous spirit.

Lead Household Well

Kingdom leaders are to lead their families effectively.—"A bishop then must be ... one who rules his own house well, having his children in submission with all reverence (for if a man does not know how to rule his own house, how will he take care of the church of God?)" (1 Tim. 3:2,4–5).

The family is at the center of God's plan for the human race. Kingdom leaders' families are to be models of what God intends the family to be. These leaders encourage their children to trust in and to follow the Lord. The children of these leaders should be known for their obedience and positive behavior. When a person cannot lead his family, he hardly can lead the church effectively.

Not a Novice

Kingdom leaders are not to be immature Christians. — "A bishop then must not be . . . a novice" (1 Tim. 3: 2, 6). Spiritual maturity has little to do with chronological age. It relates to Christian growth.

Kingdom leaders must be mature to handle the pitfalls and pressures of leadership. The heavy responsibilities of leadership place immature Christians in positions where they are vulnerable to the dangers of pride, disappointment, and frustration. Kingdom leaders know the importance of growing and maturing in their walk with the Lord.

Church leaders are not quick tempered and do not settle disputes with verbal or physical blows.

Church leaders do not spend their time in useless debates and wars of words.

Kingdom leaders are content with income adequate to meet their needs and to carry on their ministry.

Kingdom leaders' families are to be models of what God intends the family to be.

Church leaders must be mature to handle the pitfalls and pressures of leadership.

Good Testimony with Outsiders

Kingdom leaders are to have a good reputation.—Paul pointed out that a church leader *"must have a good testimony among those who are outside, lest he fall into reproach and the snare of the devil" (1 Tim. 3:7)*. The credibility of church leaders can be measured to a marked degree by the response of outsiders. The impressions of those who are not Christians about a potential leader help the church determine the integrity and character of the person.

The impressions of those who are not Christians about a potential leader help the church determine the integrity and character of the person.

To Sum Up

These qualifications for kingdom leaders represent character qualities, not skills. Persons without these traits should never be recognized by the church as kingdom leaders

First Timothy 3:1–7 is not an exhaustive list of desirable leadership qualities, but it is a healthy overview of character traits that are essential for kingdom leaders. All church leaders and potential leaders should review these qualities carefully and often. Then they can determine how well their leadership character measures up. Likewise, every church should review these qualifications often, especially when it is selecting leadership, so that it can make wise scriptural selections.

Word Pictures of Kingdom Leaders' Character

The New Testament is filled with word pictures that illustrate biblical truths and principles.

Jesus was a master of such pictures. His parables are rich with images that illustrate kingdom truths.

Second Timothy 2:1–7 presents four word pictures of kingdom leaders. Each picture illustrates the character necessary for kingdom leadership.

The Teacher

The kingdom leader is a teacher.—Kingdom leaders are teachers in the best sense of the word.

● Teachers are educators. Paul told Timothy: *"And the things that you have heard from me among*

Kingdom leaders are teachers.

many witnesses, commit these to faithful men who will be able to teach others also" (2 Tim. 2:2).

• Teachers are mentors. They are their students' wise and trusted counselors. They help students establish personal discipline and are patient in giving instruction.

• Teachers are teachable. Teachers never stop learning. They can learn from any person and circumstance.

Kingdom leaders are to help prepare the next generation for leadership. They are to mentor young leaders and are never to stop learning.

The Soldier

***The kingdom leader is like a soldier.*—**The imagery of a soldier illustrates many leadership character traits. Paul wrote: *"Endure hardship as a good soldier of Jesus Christ. No one engaged in warfare entangles himself with the affairs of this life, that he may please him who enlisted him as a soldier" (2 Tim. 2:3–4).*

• Soldiers suffer hardship. They expect adversity and are not overwhelmed when it comes.

• Soldiers are disciplined. They are separated from civilian affairs in order to focus on their duties.

• Soldiers are involved in warfare. They do not allow other activities to reduce their effectiveness.

• Soldiers are under authority. They go where they are assigned and do what they are ordered.

• Soldiers live to please their superiors. Submission to authority is a primary characteristic of soldiers.

Like good soldiers, kingdom leaders must endure hardships, live disciplined lives, concentrate on waging spiritual warfare, serve under God's authority, and live to please their Lord.

The Athlete

***Kingdom leaders are like athletes.*—**Athletics illustrates many character traits of kingdom leaders.

• Athletes compete according to the rules. Paul said, *"If anyone competes in athletics, he is not crowned unless he competes according to the rules*" (2 *Tim. 2:5*).

- Athletes are constantly in training.
- Athletes live disciplined lives.
- Athletes compete under the authority of a judge or referee.

Kingdom leaders follow God's rules, are constantly in training, and know they will give an account to God for their calling.

The Farmer

Kingdom leaders are like good farmers.—The qualities of a good farmer illustrate effective kingdom leadership. Paul explained to Timothy: *"The hardworking farmer must be first to partake of the crops"* (2 *Tim. 2:6*).

- Farmers prepare well. They must break up the soil, prepare it for planting, cultivate the crop, and be ready for the harvest.
- Farmers work hard. Farmers' days once were from sunup to sundown. With modern technology and equipment, farmers often work around the clock.
- Farmers are patient. They must wait for the seasons to arrive, the rains to come, the seed to germinate, the plants to grow, and the harvest to come.
- Farmers must seize the opportune moment. Like ancient sailors who had to be ready to catch fair winds and favorable tides, farmers must be ready when the opportune time comes to plant, cultivate, and harvest.

Likewise, kingdom leaders are to prepare well, work hard, serve patiently, and be ready for every ministry opportunity.

To Sum Up

These graphic word pictures illustrate God's clear directions for kingdom leaders' lives and calling. Kingdom leaders are to make developing these qualities their life ambition and consuming passion.

Like athletes, kingdom leaders follow God's rules, are constantly in training, and know they will give an account to God for their calling.

Like good farmers, kingdom leaders are to prepare well, work hard, serve patiently, and be ready for every ministry opportunity.

49

Such an assignment sounds impossible. Alone, it is. But kingdom leaders are not alone. God gifts and empowers them to develop these leadership qualities. He will not fail those whom He has called into His service.

Kingdom Leadership Principle Number 3

- Kingdom leadership is built on Christlike character.
- Kingdom leaders are to grow in Christlike character throughout life.
- Churches should select kingdom leaders on the basis of their Christlike character.

Kingdom Leadership Evaluation Number 3

1. What is Christ teaching you about the importance of character in kingdom leadership?
2. Where are you currently on the path of kingdom leader character development?
3. How do you measure up to the qualifications in 1 Timothy 3 and 2 Timothy 2?
4. What are your current strengths as a kingdom leader?
5. What are your current weaknesses as a kingdom leader?
6. What steps will you take to allow God to continue His work of kingdom leader character development in your life?

4

Jesus Christ: The Leader and Spiritual Conflict

"For we do not wrestle against flesh and blood, but against principalities, against powers, against the rulers of the darkness of this age, against spiritual hosts of wickedness in the heavenly places" (Eph. 6:12).

The world of Jesus' day greeted His message and commitment to His call from God with hostility. Rarely did a day or night go by when He did not face opposition and adversity. In virtually every crowd, someone questioned His motives and sought to discredit Him. He was harassed and beset with criticism and trickery without cause.

Christ was not surprised by any of this. He knew that His message and God-given calling to bring salvation to the world would evoke division and rejection. Remember He said, *"Do not think that I came to bring peace on earth. I did not come to bring peace but a sword. For I have come to 'set a man against his father, a daughter against her mother, and a daughter-in-law against her mother-in-in law'; and 'a man's foes will be those of his own household' " (Matt. 10:34–36).*

Jesus also knew that His message and commitment to His calling would bring adversity to all who followed Him. Therefore, He warned His disciples (and He warns us) to expect the same treatment He received. For *"a disciple is not above his teacher, nor a servant above his master" (Matt. 10:24).*

This must have been an unsettling moment for the disciples. To hear Jesus describe such adverse reaction to the good news of salvation must have been quite a shock. Perhaps the seriousness of their calling was never clearer than in this moment.

51

Jesus Christ and Temptation

Jesus' obedience to God's will brought the Savior face to face with temptation. Luke's Gospel tells us that *"Jesus, being filled with the Holy Spirit, returned from the Jordan and was led by the Spirit into the wilderness, being tempted for forty days by the devil" (4:1–2).*

Jesus' obedience to God's will brought the Savior face to face with temptation.

At the very beginning of Christ's ministry, the devil tempted Him to compromise His calling and to abuse His power. Satan attacked Jesus in the realm of human needs, human ambition, and human power. The devil deceptively promised the Savior things that were not his to give.

Jesus was not deceived. He resisted every temptation. As the Book of Hebrews declares, *"we do not have a High Priest who cannot sympathize with our weaknesses, but was in all points tempted as we are, yet without sin" (4:15).*

Christ withstood each temptation in the power of the Word of God.

Christ withstood each temptation in the power of the Word of God. Each time the devil assaulted Him, He replied, "It is written . . ." and quoted the Scriptures. For example, when Satan tempted Jesus to use His power to satisfy His hunger, He declared, *"It is written, 'Man shall not live by bread alone, but by every word of God' " (Luke 4:4).* The Lord's actions and words are a grand lesson in the importance of overcoming temptation with Scripture.

Jesus Christ and Opposition

Jesus faced the world's opposition as He carried out His commission. Such opposition to spiritual truth is natural and certain. Wherever the gospel is preached and taught, opposition occurs. At times this opposition is open hostility. At other times it comes in the form of internal personal resistance to the gospel.

Wherever the gospel is preached and taught, opposition occurs.

Jesus understood this truth and dealt with life-threatening opposition without once turning from His calling. Kingdom leaders likewise must be alert to this important principle and be faithful to their calling.

Christ faced unbelief.—Jesus faced unbelief about His message and His role as God's messenger. In the early days of His ministry, Jesus came to His hometown of Nazareth and preached in the synagogue. At first the people were astonished at His teachings, but they soon were offended. They rationalized about the Messenger and questioned His authority. They sarcastically asked, " *'Is this not the carpenter, the Son of Mary, and brother of James, Joses, Judas, and Simon? And are not His sisters here with us?' So they were offended at Him"* (Mark 6:3).

Mark's Gospel points out that unbelief was the real reason behind the hometown folks' negative response to Jesus. Mark wrote that Jesus *"could do no mighty work there, except that He laid his hands upon a few sick people and healed them. And He marveled because of their unbelief"* (Mark 6:5–6).

Whenever spiritual truth is declared, unbelief and rejection occur. Such unbelief caused Jesus great sadness. Matthew reported that Christ grieved over the Jewish people's unbelief. He lamented, *"O Jerusalem, Jerusalem, the one who kills the prophets and stones those who are sent to her! How often I wanted to gather your children together, as a hen gathers her chicks under her wings, but you were not willing!"* (23: 37).

Kingdom leaders must be constantly aware that some to whom the Word of God is declared will react with unbelief and rejection.

Jesus faced hatred.—Jesus experienced hatred and violence in His hometown of Nazareth. While in the synagogue, He stood up to read from the prophet Isaiah. He unrolled the scroll and found the place where it was written, *"The Spirit of the LORD is upon Me, because He has anointed Me to preach the gospel to the poor. He has sent Me to heal the brokenhearted, to preach deliverance to the captives and recovery of sight to the blind, to set at liberty those who are oppressed, to preach the acceptable year of the LORD"* (Luke 4:18–19). Then Jesus rolled up the scroll and sat down.

Jesus faced unbelief about His message and His role as God's messenger.

Whenever spiritual truth is declared, unbelief and rejection occur.

Jesus experienced hatred and violence from those who knew Him best.

53

Kingdom leaders
must remember that
when the gospel is
preached, it arouses
hatred and anger in
some people.

A long silence must have followed as the words struck home to these people with whom Jesus had grown up. He broke the silence with those stunning words: *"Today this Scripture is fulfilled in your hearing" (Luke 4:21).* Luke described the people's response: *"Then all those in the synagogue, when they heard these things, were filled with wrath, and rose up and thrust Him out of the city; and they led Him to the brow of the hill on which their city was built, that they might throw Him down over the cliff" (4:28–29).* This same story of bitter rejection is told throughout the New Testament.

Kingdom leaders must remember that when the gospel is preached, it arouses hatred and anger in some people. Therefore, leaders should expect some of the same reactions to their message.

Jesus Christ faced rejection.—Jesus went about preaching and ministering. The crowds began to grow. Some very likely came out of curiosity; some came out of sincerity; and many who heard His uncompromising message turned away. Jesus felt the pain of their rejection, but He understood that they were rejecting God's truth.

Many, who
heard Jesus'
uncompromising
message, turned
away.

John described this reaction on one occasion: *"Many of His disciples, when they heard this, said, 'This is a hard saying; who can understand it?' . . . From that time many of His disciples went back and walked with Him no more" (John 6:60,66).* Seeing these leave, Jesus turned to the twelve and asked, *"Do you also want to go away?" (John 6:67).* Peter replied with a profound truth: *"Lord, to whom shall we go? You have the words of eternal life" (John 6:68).*

The kingdom leader who declares God's truth can expect some to appear to receive the Word and later turn away. Many who seem to begin a life in the church do not finish (1 John 2:19).

Christ faced egotism.—Many times, Jesus faced those who asked for signs that would demonstrate the validity of His message. These people were arrogant, conceited, and filled with unbelief. They asked Jesus, *"What sign will You perform then, that we* *may see it and believe You?" (John 6:30).*

Kingdom leaders will experience pride and egotism as sources of opposition to God's truth.

Jesus faced legalism.—Perhaps Jesus' greatest opposition came from legalists, who were bound by ritual and tradition. Many times Jesus violated a legalistic rule or tradition. Because He refused to obey these regulations, He faced opposition. John wrote that when the Savior healed a lame man on the Sabbath, *"the Jews persecuted [him], and sought to kill Him, because He had done these things on the Sabbath. But Jesus answered them, 'My Father has been working until now, and I have been working.' Therefore the Jews sought all the more to kill Him" (John 5:16–18).*

Kingdom leaders must be prepared for God's truth to evoke opposition from legalists.

To Sum Up

Opposition to God's truth is a reality for all kingdom leaders. Jesus' life is the supreme example of that truth. Regardless of the place or culture, when God's truth is delivered by the leader God sends, opposition will occur.

Many leaders do not seem to understand that fact. They are shocked when people oppose their message. Kingdom leaders, however, must carry on the Lord's work in a world hostile to the gospel. Such opposition does not stop them from completing their mission.

Kingdom Leadership and Strongholds

Wherever God is at work, strongholds of resistance will be present. Kingdom leaders must be able to recognize these strongholds and be able to deal with them in God's power. Paul described the reality of these strongholds in 2 Corinthians 10:4–5. *"For the weapons of our warfare are not carnal but mighty in God for pulling down strongholds, casting down arguments and every high thing that exalts itself against the knowledge of God, bringing every thought into captivity to the obedience of Christ."*

Kingdom leaders will experience pride and egotism as sources of opposition to God's truth.

Kingdom leaders must be prepared for God's truth to evoke opposition from legalists.

Wherever God is at work, strongholds of resistance will be present.

Paul declared that these strongholds are those things that human reason sets against God's truth. Whenever the Word of God is proclaimed, Satan stirs up thoughts in people's minds that resist the truth. The opposition Jesus Christ experienced demonstrates this reality.

Kingdom leaders should realize that strongholds exist in the lives of people and in the church. A church may experience a stronghold from the past that resists progress. A prominent church leader may be the center of a stronghold that creates resistance to the will of God. When these strongholds are present, they block the progress of the church and hinder Christians from obeying the will of God.

Jesus Christ destroys these strongholds that stand against God's truth and work. Kingdom leaders are to use spiritual weapons that Christ provides against these strongholds.

As warriors attack and pull down city walls, kingdom leaders must attack and destroy the fortresses and arguments that resist the will of God.

"The weapons of our warfare are not carnal" (2 Cor. 10:4). The weapons we are to use are those Christ used. His weapons were the Word of God and prayer. He went against these strongholds by saying only what God said and by depending on God.

Resistance to God's work develops as soon as He begins to use individuals and churches to carry out the Great Commission. Harmful, negative arguments occur among the people. Unbelief, self-will, anger, and sometimes hatred rear their ugly heads in the church, and factions develop. All this occurs in order to resist the movement of God. Attacking and defeating these strongholds is the spiritual responsibility of every kingdom leader.

Kingdom leaders learn to recognize strongholds and destructive arguments and deal decisively with them. These leaders begin by dealing with strongholds in their own lives. They cannot deal with strongholds in others until they have

---

Whenever the Word of God is proclaimed, Satan stirs up thoughts in people's minds that resist the truth.

The weapons we are to use against strongholds are those Christ used—the Word of God and prayer.

56

dealt with strongholds within themselves. Kingdom leaders who are filled with unbelief, negative arguments, and egotism cannot effectively carry out their calling.

Kingdom Leadership Principle Number 4

- Kingdom leaders recognize the reality of opposition to the will of God.
- Kingdom leaders must identify and remove strongholds and arguments that stand against the work of God.
- Kingdom leaders must deal with personal strongholds in order to be effective leaders.

Kingdom Leadership Evaluation Number 4

1. What is the greatest temptation you currently are facing as a believer or leader?
2. What kinds of opposition are you currently facing as a believer or leader?
3. From studying Jesus' dealing with opposition, how can you apply what you have learned to dealing with opposition to your own leadership style?
4. What strongholds need to be broken down in the church you lead?
5. What are the strongholds in your life that are limiting your effectiveness as a believer or a kingdom leader?
6. What divisive arguments must be resolved in in your mind if you are to become the kingdom leader the Lord has called you to be?

Kingdom leaders learn to recognize strongholds and destructive arguments and deal decisively with them.

KINGDOM LEADER APPLICATION

Jesus Christ:
The Leader and His Competencies

“*I* *remind you to stir up the gift of God which is in you*” *(2 Tim. 1:6).*
Jesus Christ is the greatest leader of all time. He excels all others in character and purpose. His ability to deal with spiritual opposition is unequaled. He modeled ministry competencies that are crucial for kingdom leaders.

Perhaps we have read and heard such statements for so long they have lost their meaning and implications for our lives. Even so, Jesus' presence and power to restructure and redirect lives and churches are real—more real than we can imagine.

We are not talking about just the historical Christ. We are talking about the One who lives in our midst, who is capable, sensitive, and willing to empower kingdom leaders far beyond their fondest dreams.

Jesus was anointed by the Spirit and gifted by God to accomplish His mission in the world. He began His ministry with the certainty that *“the Spirit of the LORD is upon Me, because He has anointed Me to preach the gospel to the poor” (Luke 4:18).* Jesus declared, *“I do nothing of Myself; but as My Father taught Me, I speak these things” (John 8:28).*

A high level of ministry competencies is essential for kingdom leaders. These competencies are skills required to accomplish the ministry task of kingdom leader.

Jesus reminded His disciples that *"I am the vine, you are the branches. He who abides in Me, and I in him, bears much fruit; for without Me you can do nothing"* (John 15:5). Christ is the source of all competencies and the power and wisdom with which to exercise them.

Kingdom Vision

Jesus Christ was gifted with kingdom vision. He saw that His mission was to open the doors of the kingdom of God to all people. He knew His call was to do what God wanted done in the world and to bring His kingdom to completion.

The Great Commission is Christ's vision of what God wants to accomplish in the world though His people. Hence, Jesus commissioned us to *"go therefore and make disciples of all the nations, baptizing them in the name of the Father and of the Son and of the Holy Spirit, teaching them to observe all things that I have commanded you; and lo, I am with you always, even to the end of the age"* (Matt. 28:19–20).

The Great Commission is kingdom leaders' marching orders. Leaders who do not have a vision of the church as God's agent for extending His kingdom in the world will never be the force for growing churches Christ intends them to be.

Global Vision

Jesus was gifted with global vision. Although He never traveled beyond Palestine, He saw the world and what He would do in it through His disciples. Therefore, He called them to go to all nations.

Kingdom leaders must be gifted with global vision. Otherwise, their concept of what God wants them and the church to do will be far too small.

Servant Ministry

Jesus was gifted with a servant heart. He said about His ministry, *"The Son of Man did not come to be served, but to serve, and to give His life a ransom for many"* (Matt. 20:28).

> Jesus saw that His mission was to open the doors of the kingdom of God to all people.

> The Great Commission is Christ's vision of what God wants to accomplish in the world though His people.

> Kingdom leaders must be gifted with global vision.

> Kingdom leaders must be gifted by Jesus as servant leaders if they are to carry on the work He left for them to do.

Kingdom leaders are to follow the servant ministry example Jesus set. They must be gifted by Him as servant leaders if they are to carry on the work He left them to do. The picture of Jesus kneeling to wash the disciples' feet constantly reminds kingdom leaders of the importance of servant leadership.

Builder of Leaders

Jesus was a gifted leader model. He spent much of His time teaching and training leaders. He saw past their weaknesses into their hearts. He gave them a vision and drew out the best from them.

Matthew describes Jesus' calling of the initial kingdom leaders: *"And Jesus, walking beside the Sea of Galilee, saw two brothers, Simon called Peter, and Andrew his brother, … said to them, 'Follow Me, and I will make you fishers of men' "* (4:18–19). Jesus continues to call and enable leaders. That truth is evident in the growth of the church through the centuries.

Communicator

Jesus was a gifted communicator. The Gospels present Jesus as the master preacher-teacher. Matthew says that Jesus returned to Galilee when He heard John had been put in prison. And *"from that time Jesus began to preach"* (4:17).

When Jesus preached or taught, the people were astonished. They had not heard such powerful words from their teachers. When Jesus concluded the Sermon on the Mount, Matthew says, *"the people were astonished at His teaching, for He taught them as one having authority, and not as the scribes"* (7:28–29).

Spiritual Giftedness and Leadership

All kingdom leaders are called and gifted by God with competencies necessary to accomplish the work He calls them to do. The Bible records multiple examples of how God gifted His leaders. For example, following the Day of Pentecost, Peter

Jesus spent much of His time teaching and training leaders.

Jesus, the master preacher-teacher, is the model for all kingdom leaders.

All kingdom leaders are called and gifted by God with competencies necessary to accomplish the work He calls them to do.

and John were arrested for preaching. They stood before the religious leaders who had instigated Jesus' crucifixion and declared the truth about Christ. Luke records in Acts 4:13 that the religious leaders were amazed at their ability to speak about the things of God. Although the two disciples were not formally educated and trained, God gifted them to bear a mighty witness for Him.

Kingdom leaders' ability is not natural; it is supernatural. God equips them to accomplish His work. He does not gift them because of personal merit; He gifts them by His grace.

God expects kingdom leaders to exercise the gifts He gives them. Paul told Timothy to *"stir up the gift of God which is in you" (2 Tim. 1:6)*. The apostle also urged Timothy not to *"neglect the gift that is in you" (1 Tim. 4:14)*.

Every leader is accountable for using the gifts God gives him. A day of reckoning will come, and all kingdom leaders will answer to God for what they have done with their leadership gifts.

Jesus told the story of the talents to remind leaders of this truth. He said, *"For the kingdom of heaven is like a man traveling to a far country, who called his own servants and delivered his goods to them. And to one he gave five talents, to another two, and to another one, to each according to his own ability; and immediately he went on a journey" (Matt. 25:14–15)*. When the master returned, the servants were required to give an account of what they had done with their talents. Jesus then declared, *"For to everyone who has, more will be given, and he will have abundance; but from him who does not have, even what he has will be taken away" (Matt. 25:29)*.

Jesus has gifted the church to carry out the Great Commission. Paul described these spiritual gifts in the his letters to the churches. In 1 Corinthians 12:12–31, the apostle compared the church to a body that has many parts. Each part must perform its essential task for the body to

Kingdom leaders' ability is not natural; it is supernatural.

Every leader is accountable for using the gifts God gives him.

The diversity of functions in the church is reflected in its ministry gifts.

61

function properly. This diversity of functions in the church is reflected in its ministry gifts.

The Bible lists 12 ministry gifts that are given to believers in the church (1 Cor. 12:4–11,27–31; Rom. 12:4–8; Eph. 4:11). Kingdom leadership results when leaders utilize these gifts in guiding the church to accomplish the Lord's work.

Kingdom leaders need to identify and understand the gifts God has given them. The following is a brief description of each of the gifts mentioned in Paul's letters. This is not an exhaustive study. Other resources to help determine ministry giftedness are available by calling 1-800-458-2772.

> Kingdom leadership results when leaders utilize their gifts in guiding the church to accomplish the Lord's work.

Administration
1 Corinthians 12:28
"Persons gifted in the area of administration are goal- and objective-oriented. They often have strong organizational skills and are able to coordinate resources to accomplish tasks quickly. They are motivated by accomplishing desired tasks and often derive great satisfaction from viewing the results of what they have accomplished." [1]

> Persons gifted in the area of administration often have strong organizational skills and are able to coordinate resources to accomplish tasks quickly.

Evangelism
Ephesians 4:11
"Persons gifted in evangelism have a strong desire to share the gospel with nonbelievers in every situation and by all possible means. Their greatest joy in ministry is seeing the unsaved won to Christ. They have a deep desire to fulfill the Great Commission's evangelistic emphasis and prefer to devote more time and effort to the ministry of evangelism than to other church ministries that are for the edification of believers."

> Persons gifted in evangelism have a strong desire to share the gospel with nonbelievers.

Exhortation
Romans 12:8
"Persons gifted in exhortation have a special ability to encourage others in the body of Christ by giving them words of comfort, encouragement, and

> Persons gifted in exhortation have a special ability to encourage others in the body of Christ.

counsel in times of need. They are attracted to individuals seeking spiritual growth and often are willing to share their past personal failures to help motivate others toward greater spiritual maturity."

Giving
Romans 12:8
"Persons gifted in the area of giving have the ability to give material goods and financial resources with joy so that the needs of the Lord's work are met. They often can discern wise investments and usually are effective money managers. They want to give quietly and without recognition and are encouraged when they know needs are being met and prayers are being answered. These persons are more likely to give at the Lord's prompting than at human appeals. They have the ability to see financial needs others may overlook."

Persons gifted in the area of giving have the ability to give material goods and financial resources with joy.

Helps
1 Corinthians 12:28
"Persons gifted in the area of helps are motivated by a desire to further the church's ministry by meeting the needs of others, especially those in leadership positions. They enjoy giving immediate help to key individuals in order to relieve them of their financial burdens and responsibilities. While these persons are willing to do whatever is needed, they are motivated more by a desire to provide assistance than a desire to accomplish a task."

Persons gifted in the area of helps are motivated by a desire to further the church's ministry by meeting the needs of others.

Hospitality
Romans 12:13
Persons gifted in the area of hospitality have the ability to make guests feel comfortable and at home. They have a desire to provide a warm welcome to guests, whether in a ministry or a social setting. They delight in opening their homes to persons or groups and look for opportunities to

Persons gifted in the area of hospitality have a desire to provide a warm welcome to guests, whether in a ministry or a social setting.

use their gift to minister to others."

Leadership
Romans 12:8

"Persons gifted in the area of leadership have the ability to lead others toward spiritual growth. They often are considered visionary and have the ability to set goals and motivate others toward accomplishing the goals. They usually have the ability to communicate effectively to large groups of people. These persons often are chosen for leadership positions because of their ability to accomplish objectives. While giftedness in leadership is similar to giftedness in administration, persons gifted in leadership often are more concerned with the 'big picture' than with the details of accomplishing tasks."

Mercy
Romans 12:8

"Persons gifted in the area of mercy have immediate compassion for those who are suffering physically, spiritually, or emotionally. They derive great joy from meeting the needs of others and often attract people who are in distress. These persons usually need friendships in which there is deep communication and mutual commitment. They have the ability to draw out the feelings of others and are willing to be vulnerable to hurts . . . . They prefer to remove the causes of hurts rather than to look for spiritual benefits from them. Persons gifted in mercy have a tendency to avoid confrontation and firmness. They often close their spirit to those who they feel are overly harsh or critical."

Prophecy
Romans 12:6; Ephesians 4:11

"Persons gifted in the area of prophecy have the ability to proclaim God's truth without compromise. They have strong convictions, and expect

> Persons gifted in the area of leadership often are considered visionary and have the ability to set goals and motivate others toward accomplishing the goals.

> Persons gifted in the area of mercy derive great joy from meeting the needs of others and often attract people who are in distress.

> Persons gifted in the area of prophecy have the ability to proclaim God's truth without compromise.

64

others to have similar convictions. They need to express themselves verbally, especially about right and wrong. These persons may be quick to make judgments of others and quick to speak their opinions. They possess an unusual ability to discern the sincerity of others and may be painfully direct when correcting others. They are persuasive in defining right and wrong and are persistent in expressing their feelings about the need for change."

Service
Romans 12:7
"Persons gifted in the area of service have the capability to perform tasks with the joy that benefits others and meets practical needs. They may have a tendency to disregard personal health and comfort to serve others. They often have difficulty saying no when asked to serve. These persons often have an affinity for clear details and appreciate having clear instructions. They enjoy the process of serving as much as the end result and derive satisfaction from being with others who are serving."

Persons gifted in the area of service have the capability to perform tasks with the joy that benefits others and meets practical needs.

Shepherding
Ephesians 4:11
"Persons gifted in the area of shepherding have the unique ability to take responsibility for the long-term spiritual growth of a group of believers. They see guiding, feeding, and protecting a flock of Christ's followers as their responsibility. They are motivated by a desire to see those under them enjoying spiritual health and growth."

Persons gifted in the area of shepherding see guiding, feeding, and protecting a flock of Christ's followers as their responsibility.

Teaching
Romans 12:7
"Persons gifted in the area of teaching have the ability to explain God's truth so that others can understand and apply it in their lives. These persons have the desire and ability to research and present truth in an organized, systematic fashion. They are alert to details and place great emphasis

Persons gifted in the area of teaching have the ability to explain God's truth so that others can understand and apply it in their lives.

on accuracy. These persons are motivated by the desire to learn and share knowledge with others. They believe strongly in the importance of teaching as a basic foundation on which the church grows and remains faithful."

To Sum Up

Kingdom leadership is the result of divine empowerment, not human ability. Kingdom leaders live in the awareness of this truth.

Leading a church requires ministry competencies or gifts. Therefore, God never calls a church leader without gifting him for the task.

Kingdom leaders recognize the importance of ministry gifts. All adult believers should be given the opportunity to discover their gifts and to implement them in the church. More information on ministry gifts is available in *Kingdom Principles Growth Strategies*. To order, call 1-800-458-2772.

Kingdom Leadership Principle Number 5

- Kingdom leadership is the result of God-given competencies.
- Jesus Christ embodies all ministry gifts.
- Christ distributes ministry gifts to all believers.
- Kingdom leadership is God-given ability, not human ability.

Kingdom Leadership Evaluation Number 5

1. What special competencies has God given you to enable you to lead the church?
2. Which of the competencies present in Jesus Christ are present in your leadership?
3. What are your three strongest ministry gifts? Describe each one.
4. In what ways are you currently building your leadership around these strengths?
5. Identify areas of giftedness you may be neglecting in your leadership.

> Kingdom leadership is the result of divine empowerment, not human ability.

> God never calls a church leader without gifting him for the task.

KINGDOM LEADER APPLICATION

[1]All quotations in this section are from Michael Miller, *Ministry Gifts Inventory* (Nashville: Convention Press, 1995), 10–12.

Jesus Christ: The Leader and His Work

*"**I** must work the works of Him who sent Me while it is day; the night is coming when no one can work" (John 9:4).*
Jesus Christ's single-minded, unerring purpose in the world was to do the works of Him who sent Him. Even though it meant He would lay down His life for the sins of the world, Jesus focused all His energies on doing God's will.

Kingdom leaders join the Lord in His work as they guide the church in carrying out the Great Commission. To accomplish this task, leaders must carry out four basic, essential functions: *leading, administering, ministering,* and *communicating.* Jesus' example and the directions Paul gave the early churches embody these four functions (or duties) of kingdom leaders. Therefore, kingdom leaders must develop, improve, and strengthen their abilities in each of these areas.

Let us take a close look at each of these basic functions.

Leading

Leading the church to carry out the Great Commission is the principal function and responsibility of kingdom leaders. Jesus Christ is the consummate kingdom leader! He guides the church by the Holy Spirit and through His called leaders to carry out its work in the world. Paul declared, *"For as many as are led by the Spirit of God, these are sons of God" (Rom. 8:14).*

Throughout Jesus' earthly ministry, He led His disciples in their work. He sent them to preach and to heal. He directed them to feed the people who gathered to hear Him preach and teach. He commissioned them to go into all the world and preach the gospel.

The kingdom leader learns from Jesus Christ that a leader . . .

- establishes the vision,
- selects the leaders,
- trains the leaders,
- maintains a focus on the vision,
- sets a personal example, and
- watches over Christ's followers.

Leading (overseeing) is a basic kingdom leadership function. Paul pointed out this responsibility when he wrote, *"If a man desires the position of a bishop [overseer], he desires a good work" (1 Tim. 3:1).*

Jesus Christ is called an *overseer*. Peter wrote, *"but now [you] have returned to the Shepherd and Overseer of your souls" (1 Pet. 2:25).* Christ watches over His church and its work. He sees its imperfections. He knows its failures and successes. He nourishes and strengthens it for carrying out its mission.

Like Christ, a kingdom leader is an overseer. He sees the direction God is leading the church and shares what he sees with the people. He observes and guides the church's growth. He watches for spiritual problems, attacks from the devil, and compromise within the church.

The Old Testament often refers to prophets as *watchmen* (Isa. 52:8; 56:9–12; Jer. 6:17), a concept similar to the New Testament idea of an overseer. The watchman's task was to listen, watch, and warn the people. The Lord commissioned Ezekiel to *"hear a word from My mouth, and give them warning from Me" (Ezek. 3:17).* Like watchmen, kingdom leaders hear from God and warn the people.

The kingdom leader watches over the spiritual condition of the church and the progress the church is making in carrying out the Great Commission. Paul reminded the elders from Ephesus to *"take heed to yourselves and to all the flock, among which the Holy Spirit has made you overseers, to shepherd the church of God which He purchased with His own blood" (Acts 20:28).*

> *Leading (overseeing) is a basic kingdom leadership function.*

> Like watchmen, kingdom leaders hear from God and warn the people.

The kingdom leader is accountable to Jesus Christ for overseeing the church. The Book of Hebrews encourages believers to remember that their leaders *"watch out for your souls, as those who must give account" (Heb. 13:17)*.

Church members must find in their leaders a lifestyle worthy of being emulated. Jesus called on people to follow His example (Matt. 4:19). Paul urged Christians to imitate his lifestyle (1 Cor. 11:1). All kingdom leaders must be able to encourage the churches they lead to duplicate their walk with God. Paul told Timothy to *"be an example to the believers in word, in conduct, in love, in spirit, in faith, in purity" (1 Tim. 4:12)*.

Leading includes vision, oversight, and personal example. Every kingdom leader must strive to excel in this function of leadership.

Administering

Jesus Christ, the Ruler of the kingdom of God and the church, the "KING OF KINGS AND LORD OF LORDS" (Rev. 19:16), was a master administrator. He understood His disciples' character and personality. He chose and called them. He knew that, by His grace, they would accomplish the work He gave them to do. Jesus assigned these disciples their mission tasks and followed up on their assignments when they returned.

Administering is a basic kingdom leadership function. The biblical term *elder* describes the kingdom leader's administrative work.

During the New Testament era, synagogues had rulers called elders. Generally, these were older, distinguished men who were appointed to lead the people.

The New Testament calls pastors elders. The term *elder* does not describe a separate category of church leaders. It describes a function of the kingdom leader.

The kingdom leader is accountable to Jesus Christ for overseeing the church.

Leading includes vision, oversight, and personal example.

Administering is a basic kingdom leadership function.

The elder directs the work of the church. Paul told Titus to *"appoint elders in every city" (Titus 1:5)*. The apostle described elders as overseers (Acts 20:28). To "oversee" is to direct, guide, or manage the church. The pastor-leader is to manage, delegate, and prioritize the church's work.

Kingdom leaders administer the work of church and equip the saints for ministry. Equipping the church requires management and delegation. These roles are part of the leader's administrative function.

The kingdom leader discovers needs and matches the church's resources to the needs. They administer these resources according to priorities adopted by the congregation. This enables the church to carry out the Great Commission effectively.

Ministering

Jesus Christ modeled the importance of the kingdom leadership function of ministry. He said that *"the Son of Man did not come to be served, but to serve, and to give His life a ransom for many" (Matt. 20:28)*.

Jesus began His Galilean ministry by declaring that God had sent Him *"to heal the brokenhearted, to proclaim liberty to the captives and recovery of sight to the blind, to set at liberty those who are oppressed" (Luke 4:18)*.

As the Good Shepherd, Jesus is the ideal model of leadership ministry. Peter referred to Him as *"the Chief Shepherd" (1 Pet. 5:4)*. Paul called church leaders *pastors* (Eph. 4:11), a word that means "shepherd." This word is used often in the New Testament to describe the work of the local church leader.

The shepherd analogy is an excellent illustration of ministry. Shepherds feed, lead, protect, and watch over the sheep. As the shepherd of the church, the pastor must feed, lead, protect, and watch over the congregation.

Communicating

Jesus Christ is the perfect model of a kingdom communicator. The Gospels declare that *"Jesus came to Galilee, preaching the gospel of the kingdom of God" (Mark 1:14)* and *"Jesus went about all Galilee, teaching in their synagogues" (Matt. 4:23).*

Jesus was a preacher and teacher. His ministry was centered around effectively communicating God's message.

Preaching is a basic part of the kingdom leader's role as a communicator. He is the *kerux*, the herald of God's message. He is responsible for proclaiming the Word. Paul said to Timothy, *"Preach the word!" (2 Tim. 4:2).* Kingdom leaders must work throughout their ministry to improve this gift.

Teaching is a basic role in the kingdom leader's function as a communicator. Kingdom leaders must be *"able to teach" (1 Tim. 3:2).* They must teach the Scriptures with authority. Paul said, *"These things command and teach" (1 Tim. 4:11).*

Kingdom leaders are to mentor future leaders. Paul reminded Timothy that *"the things that you have heard from me among many witnesses, commit these to faithful men who will be able to teach others also" (2 Tim. 2:2).* Just as Jesus mentored His disciples, mature kingdom leaders have the responsibility of mentoring future kingdom leaders.

Kingdom leaders are responsible for other types of communication within the church. Paul told Timothy, *"All Scripture is given by inspiration of God, and is profitable for doctrine, for reproof, for correction, for instruction in righteousness" (2 Tim. 3:16).*

Kingdom leaders are responsible for reproving, both privately and publicly, individual believers who need correction. Paul instructed Timothy to *"in humility [correct] those who are in opposition, if God perhaps will grant them repentance, so that they may know the truth, and that they may come to their senses*

Preaching and teaching are basic roles in the kingdom leader's function as a communicator.

and escape the snare of the devil, having been taken captive by him to do his will" (2 Tim. 2:25–26). Leaders also are responsible for using the Scripture to correct the church if and when it moves into error.

The kingdom leader is a preacher and teacher. He must communicate the Word of God to the church. He must encourage, reprove, and correct. Often this is not easy. Nevertheless, communication is a biblical function entrusted to kingdom leaders.

Definition of a Kingdom Leader

Jesus Christ is the model all kingdom leaders must emulate. He exemplified the truth that calling, character, and competencies are foundational to effective leadership. He functioned as leader, administrator, minister, and communicator of the Word of God.

In light of Jesus' teachings and example, . . .
a kingdom leader can be defined as a person called by God to follow Christ in a life of discipleship, utilizing the leadership gifts given by the Holy Spirit to lead the church in carrying out the Great Commission for the purpose of expanding the kingdom of God.

Kingdom Leadership Principle Number 6

- Kingdom leadership grows out of God's call.
- Kingdom leadership is shaped by character.
- Kingdom leadership is accomplished by God-given competencies.
- Kingdom leadership guides the church to achieve the Great Commission.
- Kingdom leadership focuses on the expansion of the kingdom of God.
- The four functions of kingdom leaders are:
  Leading
  Administering
  Ministering
  Communicating

The kingdom leader must communicate the Word of God to the church.

A kingdom leader is a person called by God to follow Christ in a life of discipleship, utilizing the leadership gifts given by the Holy Spirit to lead the church in carrying out the Great Commission for the purpose of expanding the kingdom of God.

Kingdom leadership includes four functions:
Leading
Administering
Ministering
Communicating

Kingdom Leadership Evaluation
Number 6

1. Identify God's call in your life.
2. How is God working to develop your character?
3. What competencies has God given you to equip you for leadership?
4. Which functions identified in this chapter need improvement in your ministry?
5. Which leadership functions identified in this chapter are strengths in your ministry?

K
I
N
G
D
O
M

L
E
A
D
E
R

A
P
P
L
I
C
A
T
I
O
N

THE KINGDOM LEADERSHIP PATH

Discovering the Leader's Place on the Journey

*"**E**nter by the narrow gate; for wide is the gate and broad is the way that leads to destruction, and there are many who go in by it. Because narrow is the gate and difficult is the way which leads to life, and there are few who find it" (Matt. 7:13–14).*

The Path of Life
We are confronted with many options and make many choices in life. The most important choice we make is the path on which to live our lives.

God calls us to walk the path that leads to life. Jesus spoke of two paths people travel. One leads to life; the other leads to destruction. Everyone chooses a path. Believers in Christ choose the path of life. The psalmist declared, *"You will show me the path of life; in Your presence is fullness of joy; at Your right hand are pleasures forevermore" (Ps. 16:11).*

The path of life is filled with joy. The thrill of knowing God and being loved by Him gladdens the heart. In spite of adversities, satisfaction and fulfillment come to those who walk this path. Many distractions will come along the way, but believers can walk the path of life in perfect peace.

Obedience to God's Word prevents believers from wandering from the path of life. The Book of Proverbs says, *"He who keeps instruction is in the way of life, but he who refuses reproof goes astray" (10:17).*

The believer who walks the path of life learns wisdom from the Word of God. The Book of Proverbs declares of wisdom, *"Her ways are ways of pleasantness, and all her paths are peace" (3:17).* Righteousness, joy, and peace are the rewards of traveling the path of life.

Sojourners with God

Throughout Scripture, believers are portrayed as sojourners with God. This biblical image of sojourners is significant for kingdom leaders. Abraham modeled the sojourning nature of the journey to which God calls believers. The Bible says, *"By faith Abraham obeyed when he was called to go out to the place which he would afterward receive as an inheritance. And he went out, not knowing where he was going. By faith he sojourned in the land of promise as in a foreign country, dwelling in tents"* (Heb. 11:8–9). Like Abraham, sojourners walk by faith. They follow wherever God leads.

The Book of Hebrews says of those who walked by faith: *"These all died in faith, not having received the promises, but having seen them afar off were assured of them, embraced them and confessed that they were strangers and pilgrims on the earth"* (Heb. 11:13). These believers were travelers on the path of life, following God wherever He led them.

Believers on the path of life are to abstain from things that would distract them or slow their progress. Peter said, *"Beloved, I beg you as sojourners and pilgrims, abstain from fleshly lusts which war against the soul"* (1 Pet. 2:11).

Sojourners travel a well-worn road. The Old Testament word for "path" describes a well-worn footpath. Many have traveled the path that leads to life. God's Word tells us about those who have gone before and the peace and joy they experienced on that path.

Sojourners experience dangers that lie along the path of life. In the midst of these obstacles, however, believers, like Abraham, confidently move forward by faith.

Jesus Christ and the Leadership Path

Jesus was a trailblazer. He opened a new and living way to God. He made access to God possible through His death on the cross. He stands for all time as *"the way, the truth, and the life"* (John 14:6).

Believers are sojourners with God.

Like Abraham, sojourners walk by faith.

Believers on the path of life are to abstain from things that would distract them or slow their progress.

Sojourners experience both dangers and joys on the path of life.

76

Jesus came to complete the work that God gave Him to do, and His path led to Calvary. He said, *"I have glorified You on the earth. I have finished the work which You have given Me to do" (John 17:4).*

Throughout His life, Jesus focused on the path He was to follow all the way to His death. Finally, on the cross He bowed His head and said, *"It is finished!" (John 19:30).* Jesus truly models the importance of being obedient to the will of God even unto death.

The kingdom leader learns many valuable lessons from Christ. First, God calls each leader to walk a specific leadership path. Second, each kingdom leader must set as his goal finishing what God called him to do. Third, kingdom leaders become lifelong learners and continue to grow while on the leadership path.

The Kingdom Leadership Path
Kingdom leaders are called to walk a path that is different from that of other believers. They are called to a kingdom leadership journey. God has designed this path for each individual leader, and His design accomplishes His purposes for His kingdom and the church.

Each plateau on the kingdom leadership path is illustrated by graphics on the following pages, and the entire leadership path appears at the end of the book.

Perhaps the clearest picture of the leadership path is given by the apostle Paul. He described the leadership path as a racecourse. When writing to Timothy he said, *"I have fought the good fight, I have finished the race, I have kept the faith" (2 Tim. 4:7).* The word translated *race* actually means "course." God places the leader on a leadership path or course in order for him to accomplish what he has been called to do.

God calls each leader to walk a specific leadership path.

Kingdom leaders are called to walk a path that is different from other believers.

Each kingdom leader must set as his goal finishing what God called him to do.

The kingdom leadership path varies from leader to leader.

77

The Nature of the Leadership Path

The kingdom leadership path varies from leader to leader. God designs a leadership path for every kingdom leader. Paul said, *"But none of these things move me; nor do I count my life dear to myself, so that I may finish my race with joy, and the ministry which I received from the Lord Jesus, to testify to the gospel of the grace of God" (Acts 20:24).* Paul understood that God had given him a path to follow. His goal was to finish the course, regardless of the dangers that stood in his way.

Personal Path

The kingdom leadership path is designed by God for each individual leader. Paul's course was that of an apostle. Others' paths were to be that of an evangelist or pastor. Paul's leadership path led him to establish many churches and eventually led him to Rome. The paths of other early apostles led to other places and other work.

God calls out kingdom leaders to guide the church in carrying out the Great Commission. He plans a path for them to follow as they lead the church forward. This path is designed around the ministry responsibility God gives to the kingdom leader. Paul speaks of his work as *"the ministry which I received from the Lord Jesus" (Acts 20:24).*

Path of Perseverance

Throughout Paul's ministry, he expressed fear of failing to finish his leadership path. He wrote in Galatians, *"lest by any means I might run, or had run, in vain" (2:2).* He also wrote in Philippians, *"that I may rejoice in the day of Christ that I have not run in vain or labored in vain" (2:16).* The apostle told the Philippian Christians, *"forgetting those things which are behind and reaching forward to those things which are ahead, I press toward the goal for the prize of the upward call of God in Christ Jesus" (Phil. 3:13–14).*

Paul realized his ministry would be in vain if he did not remain faithful to God. Therefore, he

---

God calls each kingdom leader to a path that is personally designed for him.

This path is designed around the ministry responsibilities God gives the kingdom leader.

Each kingdom leader is to walk faithfully the path God called him to.

pressed toward the prize of his high calling in Christ Jesus. He focused on completing his course.

Throughout his ministry, Paul was obedient to God's call to be the apostle to the Gentiles. Like Paul, all kingdom leaders must be obedient to God's call and to the leadership path He has for them. Remember Jesus' words: *"No one, having put his hand to the plow, and looking back, is fit for the kingdom of God" (Luke 9:62).*

Path of Adversity

Kingdom leaders learn from Paul that adversity and difficulty are scattered along the leadership path. He described the pressures and troubles he faced on the path: *"We are hard pressed on every side, yet not crushed; we are perplexed, but not in despair; persecuted, but not forsaken; struck down, but not destroyed. . . . For we who live are always delivered to death for Jesus' sake, that the life of Jesus also may be manifested in our mortal flesh. So then death is working in us, but life in you. . . . Therefore we do not lose heart. Even though our outward man is perishing, yet the inward man is being renewed day by day. . . . while we do not look at the things which are seen, but at the things which are not seen" (2 Cor. 4:8–9, 11–12, 16, 18).*

Leaders are pressed on every side, but not crushed. They are perplexed, but not in despair; persecuted, but not forsaken; struck down, but not destroyed. Death works in the leader, but life results in the churches. Leaders don't lose heart. Leaders see the unseen, the eternal.

Difficulty and adversity lie along the leadership path, but God assures victory to leaders who walk this path by faith. Paul said it best: *"For all things are for your sakes, that grace, having spread through the many, may cause thanksgiving to abound to the glory of God" (2 Cor. 4:15).* Adversity on the leadership path results in glory to God.

Path of Development

As kingdom leaders move along the leadership

Adversity and difficulty are scattered along the leadership path.

God assures victory to leaders who walk the kingdom leadership path by faith.

79

path, growth and development become important. Paul said, *"Do you not know that those who run in a race all run, but one receives the prize? Run in such a way that you may obtain it. And everyone who competes for the prize is temperate in all things. Now they do it to obtain a perishable crown, but we for an imperishable crown. Therefore I run thus: not with uncertainty. Thus I fight: not as one who beats the air. But I discipline my body and bring it into subjection, lest, when I have preached to others, I myself should become disqualified"* (1 Cor. 9:24–27).

Path of Reward

Those who are on the kingdom leadership path must focus on the goal. Discipline and stamina assure the leader's effectiveness throughout the leadership journey.

The kingdom leader will be rewarded for his work. The reward at the end of the journey makes the struggle bearable. In discouraging times, the only thing that may keep a leader on the path is his call to leadership and the prize that awaits him at the end of the way.

Leadership Path Plateaus

As kingdom leaders progress along the leadership path, they arrive at various plateaus. These plateaus are arrival points along the path. They identify points of accomplishment and allow for rest, review, and reflection. These leadership plateaus could be compared to stopover points on a foot-trail.

Specific plateaus in each kingdom leader's life vary. Some leaders will remain at one leadership plateau longer than others. Because God has designed a personal leadership path for each kingdom leader, the movement from one plateau to another and the length of time on each plateau varies among leaders.

Kingdom leaders must be aware of their progress along the leadership path. Paul never

> Those who are on the kingdom leadership path must focus on the goal.

> As kingdom leaders progress along the leadership path, they arrive at various leadership plateaus.

> Because God has designed a personal leadership path for each kingdom leader, the movement from one plateau to another and the length of time on each plateau varies among leaders.

doubted where he was going on the path God had designed for him. As he testified before King Agrippa, he said, *"I was not disobedient to the heavenly vision" (Acts 26:19)*. Paul maintained awareness of the course that God had laid out for him as a kingdom leader, even when he was in difficult circumstances. All kingdom leaders should maintain the same perception concerning their progress on the leadership journey.

By examining his leadership journey, the kingdom leader will discover where he is in his pilgrimage. As a result of this discovery, a plan can be designed for progressing on the leadership path.

The kingdom leadership path has six specific plateaus. Though these plateaus may appear on the diagram to be sequential, a leader may move from one plateau to another in a nonsequential route. For some leaders, two or more of these plateaus may occur at the same time. Other leaders may experience additional plateaus beyond those that are identified in the diagram.

The Beginning Leader
The beginning leader is identifying the various aspects of kingdom leadership. At this plateau, a leader has a clear sense of God's call to leadership. When Paul was called, he responded to God's direction in his life (Acts. 9:15–16). He wrote the Galatian Christians: *"But when it pleased God, who separated me from my mother's womb and called me through His grace, to reveal . . . Him among the Gentiles" (1:15–16).*

The beginning leader spends serious time in prayer and Bible study in order to clarify the type of leadership to which God is calling him. He undertakes an earnest evaluation of what God is saying about his call to leadership. Paul first consulted

The kingdom leadership path has six specific plateaus.

A leader may move from one plateau to another in a nonsequential route.

The beginning leader spends serious time in prayer and Bible study in order to clarify the type of leadership to which God is calling him.

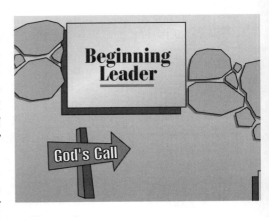

Beginning
kingdom leaders
are starting to
function as
recognized
leaders in the
church.

Beginning leaders
experience the
challenges of
leadership for the
first time.

Coming to the
realization that God
actually has called
him to lead the
church is an exciting
and emotionally
stirring time for the
beginning leader.

The assimilating
leader is rapidly
absorbing vast
amounts of
information about
his role as a leader.

the Lord concerning his call to leadership. He said, *"I did not immediately confer with flesh and blood, nor did I go up to Jerusalem to those who were apostles before me; but I went to Arabia, and returned again to Damascus" (Gal. 1:16–17)*. All beginning leaders should follow the apostle's example.

Beginning kingdom leaders are starting to function as recognized leaders in the church. When Paul received God's call, he began to exercise his leadership ability. Acts states, *"Immediately he preached the Christ in the synagogues, that He is the Son of God" (Acts 9:20)*. God gifts the beginning leader to lead, and he begins to give evidence of his call by using his gifts.

Beginning leaders experience the challenges of leadership for the first time. Whether it is preaching, teaching, or leading a committee meeting, the beginning leader is discovering the basic responsibilities of leadership.

Beginning leaders live in the romance of leadership. Things are bright, optimistic, and ideal to the beginning leader. Coming to the realization that God actually has called him to lead the church is an exciting and emotionally stirring time.

Beginning leaders are naive about many troublesome issues. They are not aware that some people in the church have personal agendas. They may be shocked by the kinds of things that sometimes go on behind the closed doors of committee meetings and among other so-called leaders of the church.

God's call is the beginning point on the leadership path. Some beginning leaders may be considerably older than others. Some may have more formal education than others. All beginning leaders, however, share many of the same characteristics in the early days of their leadership.

The Assimilating Leader

The assimilating leader is rapidly absorbing vast

amounts of information about his role as a leader. This plateau describes a person whose learning curve is incredibly high. Whether receiving formal education or on-the-job experience, the assimilating leader is full of questions. He is exploring the parameters of kingdom leadership and getting comfortable with his leadership role.

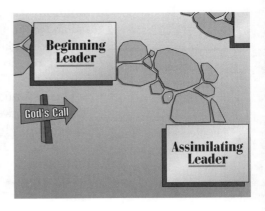

The assimilating leader continues to make spiritual progress. Paul experienced this plateau. Luke records, *"But Saul increased all the more in strength, and confounded the Jews who dwelt in Damascus, proving that this Jesus is the Christ" (Acts 9:22).*

Personal development as a leader is directly related to spiritual growth and maturity. The assimilating leader continues to evaluate God's call. He develops a growing awareness of the character God is developing in his life. At this plateau, he is growing in his understanding of the God-given competencies provided him for leadership.

The assimilating leader often faces his first crisis in ministry. This crisis may come in the form of criticism or personal troubles. At this plateau, the leader may experience for the first time real opposition to the gospel and kingdom leadership. Paul faced such an experience in his ministry. Acts 9:23 says, *"Now after many days were past, the Jews plotted to kill him."* Regardless of the nature of the crisis, the leader must, with God's guidance, deal with the issue.

The assimilating leader develops new relationships with other kingdom leaders. After three years of work, Paul developed a relationship with Peter that would be a source of encouragement to Paul in later years (Gal. 1:18–19).

The assimilating leader is not well known by other churches. At this plateau of leadership, Paul was not recognized by the churches and other

> The assimilating leader is exploring the parameters of kingdom leadership and getting comfortable with his leadership role.

> The assimilating leader is growing in his understanding of the competencies God has given him.

> The assimilating leader often faces his first crisis in ministry.

kingdom leaders. He said, *"And I was unknown by face to the churches of Judea which were in Christ"* (Gal. 1:22). Assimilating leaders are just beginning to establish relationships, but they soon discover the importance of relationships to leadership.

The assimilating leader becomes aware of the distance between the ideal and the realities of leadership. He may believe the church ought to function on biblical principles, but he is aware that many times the church is far from that standard. This is a critical plateau in the life of a leader.

The Building Leader

The leader who arrives at the building plateau is extending his leadership influence. He begins to develop a strategy of leadership. He is experiencing the privilege of having the church respond to his leadership. His accomplishments are increasing at this plateau.

Building leaders become aware of the power of influence in leadership. Fourteen years passed before Paul was recognized as a strong, influential leader. He wrote, *"Then after fourteen years I went up again to Jerusalem . . . and communicated to them that gospel which I preach among the Gentiles, but privately to those who were of reputation, lest by any means I might run, or had run, in vain"* (Gal. 2:1–2). Paul went to Jerusalem to discuss with Peter and the other apostles the conversion of the Gentiles. The building leader respects the influence that comes from being a kingdom leader. However, he is careful to remain aware that this influence comes from God, not from the leader's personal abilities.

At this plateau, the leader is expanding his influence. Paul wrote that the churches of Judea did

The assimilating leader becomes aware of the growing distance between the ideal and the realities of leadership.

The building leader begins to develop a strategy of leadership.

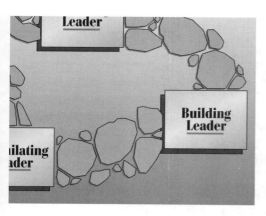

Building leaders become aware of the power of influence in leadership.

84

not know him. *"They were hearing only, 'He who formerly persecuted us now preaches the faith which he once tried to destroy.' And they glorified God"* (Gal. 1:23–24). The report of God's work in Paul's life brought joy to the church. Churches will recognize and appreciate God's blessings on the kingdom leader's life and work. They recognize him as a leader and become aware of his growing influence at this plateau.

The church at Antioch recognized the leadership gifts of Barnabas and Paul. Acts records that *"as they ministered to the Lord and fasted, the Holy Spirit said, 'Now separate to Me Barnabas and Saul for the work to which I have called them.' Then, having fasted and prayed, and laid hands on them, they sent them away"* (Acts 13:2–3). The church's recognition of kingdom leaders enables them to extend the influence of their leadership.

The building leader experiences the thrill of achievement and fulfillment. As the leader uses his God-given leadership gifts to assist the church in carrying out the Great Commission, he discovers the wonderful thrill of accomplishment. Paul had these same experiences (Acts 13:48–49; 14:21–22, 27). The victories of leadership are significant for the building leader. They bring greater confidence and confirm that God is using the leader in the church.

The building leader experiences the trials of leadership. Many times the trials are greater at this plateau than at any other. Troubles can be a source of discouragement. They also can build stronger character and commitment to God's call. Paul dealt with trials in his life at this plateau of leadership. *"The Jews stirred up the devout and prominent women and the chief men of the city, raised up persecution against Paul and Barnabas, and expelled them from their region"* (Acts 13:50).

The building leader begins to develop his personal leadership style and routines. His unique approach to the ministry begins to take shape. Some of the routines are good and beneficial; others may create difficulties. Paul practiced a routine in every new city he entered by going first to a synagogue to preach and teach (Acts 13:5).

The building leader is energized by the great needs that appear all around him. He faces the struggle between expanding opportunities for service and lack of time to accomplish all his plans. He soon discovers that the leadership journey involves more than influence, and that discovery leads him to the next plateau.

The Achieving Leader

This plateau sets the stage for the kingdom leader's future growth and development. Through good and bad experiences, this plateau provides the achieving leader opportunities to integrate his leadership style, accomplishments, and the lessons learned on the leadership path.

The achieving leader receives growing recognition for leadership and ministry accomplishments.

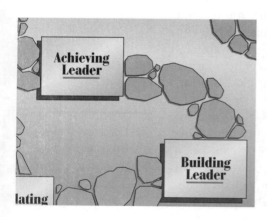

Paul wrote about his meeting with the other apostles on the difficult issue of the gospel being preached to the Gentiles: *"When James, Cephas, and John, who seemed to be pillars, perceived the grace that had been given to me, they gave me and Barnabas the right hand of fellowship, that we should go to the Gentiles"* (Gal. 2:9).

Achieving leaders are respected by their peers and stand out as those who can be counted on in difficult times. At this plateau, the leader is focused on consistency in leadership and ministry and shows Christlike character.

The achieving leader helps develop emerging kingdom leaders. He learns to integrate the lessons of leadership and shares them with a new generation of leaders. Luke wrote that Paul and

Barnabas *"remained in Antioch, teaching and preaching the word of the Lord, with many others"* (Acts 15:35).

Perhaps one of the greatest achievements of leadership is mentoring new leaders. The church relies on its mature leaders to mentor the new leaders God raises up (2 Tim. 2:2). Paul spent much time developing emerging leaders. Acts 16:1,3 states that Paul *"came to Derbe and Lystra. And behold, a certain disciple was there, named Timothy. . . . Paul wanted to have him go on with him."*

The achieving leader is aware of personal limitations and the need for more workers to carry out the Great Commission. He has the ability to identify potential ministry leaders.

The achieving leader has developed the ability to handle crises in the church. Paul demonstrated this competency when he dealt with the apostles concerning the gospel being preached to the Gentiles (Gal. 2:2).

> The achieving leader learns to integrate the lessons of leadership and shares them with a new generation of leaders.

> The maturing leader focuses on multiplying his efforts through others.

The Maturing Leader

The maturing leader focuses on multiplying his efforts through others. This leader has moved beyond the need to receive credit for all the work. He understands the great importance of coworkers in carrying out the Great Commission. The maturing leader is characterized by years of service, experience, and accomplishments in ministry.

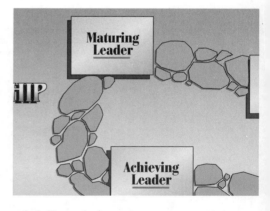

The maturing leader clearly senses where God is leading the church and him in his personal ministry. Paul listened carefully to the Lord and followed His directions. Acts says, *"Now when they had gone through Phrygia and the region of Galatia, they were forbidden by the Holy Spirit to preach the word in Asia. After they had come to Mysia, they tried to go into Bithynia, but the Spirit did not permit them. . . . Now after he*

> The maturing leader clearly senses where God is leading him and the church .

had seen the vision, immediately we sought to go to Macedonia, concluding that the Lord had called us to preach the gospel to them" (16:6–7,10).

The maturing leader is a crisis-tested leader. He knows from experience that leaders will have trials and adversities to overcome. He has experienced many ordeals in leadership and has developed appropriate responses to them.

The maturing leader spends greater amounts of time with beginning, assimilating, and building leaders. Leaders who are at these earlier plateaus on the leadership path look to mature leaders for direction and counsel. Paul was surrounded by these kinds of leaders at this plateau on his leadership path (Acts 20:4).

The Refocusing Leader

The refocusing leader is evaluating his past and future work as a kingdom leader. This leader has served many years and accomplished much. He is mature and established in leadership style and influence. He is respected by his peers and senses that God is leading him in a new direction.

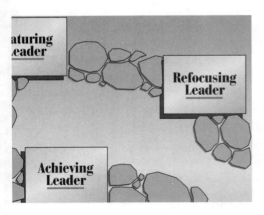

Paul spoke with the Ephesian elders about this plateau in his own life: *"You know, from the first day that I came to Asia, in what manner I always lived among you, serving the Lord with all humility, with many tears and trials . . . how I kept back nothing that was helpful, but . . . publicly and from house to house, testifying to Jews, and also to Greeks, repentance toward God. . . . But none of these things move me; nor do I count my life dear to myself, so that I may finish my race with joy, and the ministry which I received from the Lord Jesus"* (Acts 20:18–21,24).

The refocusing leader is adjusting to the changes in his leadership. Once Paul traveled widely, planting churches. Later, he knew he was

The maturing leader knows from experience that leaders have to overcome trials and adversities.

The refocusing leader is evaluating his past and future work as a kingdom leader.

to face prison and death in order to accomplish the work God had given him to do.

The apostle learned at the refocusing plateau to concentrate on what God had given him to do. All kingdom leaders must do the same. The leadership path leads in many directions. Each leader must remain close to God so that he can know the direction God is leading him.

The refocusing leader is adjusting to the changes in his leadership.

The refocusing leader is respected as a leader of leaders. His reputation and character are highly esteemed. He consults with young leaders and encourages them to develop their own leadership competencies. Paul said in his good-bye to the Ephesian elders, *"Therefore take heed to yourselves and to all the flock, among which the Holy Spirit has made you overseers, to shepherd the church of God"* (Acts 20:28).

The refocusing leader is respected as a leader of leaders.

The refocusing leader wants to finish the leadership path as strongly as he began. He isn't interested in quitting short of the goal. He is committed to finishing the work God called him to do. He knows his time for leadership is almost over. Nevertheless, he remains faithful to his God-called task in whatever circumstances he finds himself.

Paul remained busy at his work until God called him home. Acts 28:30–31 states that *"Paul dwelt two whole years in his own rented house, and received all who came to him, preaching the kingdom of God and teaching the things which concern the Lord Jesus Christ with all confidence, no one forbidding him."*

The refocusing leader is committed to finishing the work God has called him to do.

To Sum Up

Leadership plateaus are points of rest and reflection. The kingdom leader needs to pause at each plateau to assess his calling, character development, and competencies. These interludes also afford the leader the opportunity to look forward and determine where God is directing him on the leadership path.

Leadership plateaus are points of rest and reflection.

Kingdom Leader Evaluation Number 7

1. Where are you currently on the leadership path?
2. How long have you been at this particular point?
3. What steps should you take to move to the next plateau on the path?
4. At this point on the leadership path, are you reflecting on God's call in your life? If so, how?
5. What elements of character is God developing in you at this particular point on the path?
6. Which of your leadership competencies need immediate attention at this point on the leadership path?
7. Which competencies need long-range attention?

8

KINGDOM LEADER LIFE APPLICATION

Regardless of where a leader may be on the leadership path, whether at the beginning or the refocusing plateau, Jesus Christ is the leader's ever-present guide and strength.

Jesus calls leaders and gives them power to follow in His steps. He gives leaders the legacy of faithfulness and a heritage of unwavering empowerment.

When the Lord calls a kingdom leader, He commissions him to lead His people to carry out the Great Commission. That commission is a sacred trust between the leader and the Lord as well as between the leader and those who follow him. Without this sacred trust, kingdom leadership is lost, and the leadership task becomes nothing more than a management and administrative function. That does not qualify as kingdom leadership.

Christ has clear, unmistakable words of hope and counsel for each generation of kingdom leaders. His words remind each generation of leaders that they carry a tremendous responsibility in the church. Jesus' final words to the first kingdom leaders embody His counsel for each successive generation of leaders. No matter what cultural or social trends or upheavals may come, these eternal truths remain. Every leader should listen attentively to the words of the greatest leader who will ever live—Jesus Christ, our Lord, our leader.

The night before Jesus faced sacrificing Himself on the cross for the sins of the world, He gathered His disciples for a final Passover meal. These men had been with Him throughout His earthly ministry. They had traveled and eaten with Him. They had heard His profound teachings and had witnessed His mighty power. Now He was talking about leaving them. His shocking words brought grave concern to their hearts and minds.

During the Passover meal, Jesus announced that one of the group was a traitor. This only added to the disciples' distress. They were full of questions and anxiety. They began to ask, *"Lord, is it I?" (Matt. 26:22).*

These disciples were about to begin their mission as kingdom leaders in a world hostile to God and the gospel. To learn that Jesus would not be present with them was traumatic.

Jesus reassured and encouraged them at this difficult moment. His words, recorded in John 14–16, are a comfort and a challenge to every God-called kingdom leader. Every leader should write them on his heart.

Do Not Be Troubled

Jesus could see the concern and anxiety in His disciples' faces. He urged them to trust Him and to look ahead. He said, *"Let not your heart be troubled; you believe in God, believe also in Me. . . . I go to prepare a place for you. And if I go and prepare a place for you, I will come again and receive you to Myself; that where I am, there you may be also" (John 14:1–3).* These disciples needed encouragement, a reason to continue. They easily could have given up, but Jesus calmed their fears.

Kingdom leaders must put their faith in Christ. Nothing else and no one else will do. Without confidence in Christ, kingdom service is impossible. Regardless of the difficulties kingdom leaders face, Jesus urges them to put their faith in Him and not to be troubled.

I Will Come Again

Nothing could have brought greater grief to the disciples than to know that Jesus was going to leave. Being left without Him was a terrible plight. Many questions came to their minds. Where was He going? Would He return? Would they be left

---

Regardless of where a leader may be on on the leadership path, whether at the beginning or at the refocusing plateau, Jesus Christ is the leader's ever-present guide and strength.

Without confidence in Christ, kingdom service is impossible.

Though kingdom leaders sometimes may feel alone and separated from Jesus, He will come again.

alone? His assurance that he would return was an immediate source of encouragement. It made His departure bearable. His coming again meant that He would continue to be their Lord and leader.

Today Jesus speaks to kingdom leaders who are anxiously working in lonely, dangerous, difficult places. He promises them, *"I will come again" (John 14:3)*. His coming again means unbroken fellowship. Kingdom leaders sometimes feel alone and separated from Jesus, but they can take comfort in the knowledge that He will come again.

I Will Bless Your Work

The disciples must have wondered how the work Jesus started would continue. Perhaps they whispered to one another, "How can we continue this work without Jesus?" Where would they find the direction and strength to finish the work He had entrusted to them? Jesus promised, *"Most assuredly, I say to you, he who believes in Me, the works that I do he will do also; and greater works than these he will do, because I go to My Father" (John 14:12)*.

These leaders must have been shocked at what Jesus said. His work not only would continue, it would be greater than ever. His promise to these leaders speaks to the heart of every generation of leaders. His work will not fail. It will continue to grow.

All kingdom leaders are called to do the work of Christ—to lead the church to carry out the Great Commission. And He promises to bless them in this mighty work.

I Will Do What You Ask

Jesus assured the disciples of His continued presence and support. He encouraged them to ask for His help and promised to do what they asked in His name. He said, *"Whatever you ask in My name, that I will do, that the Father may be glorified in the Son" (John 14:13)*.

Jesus wants His present-day leaders to ask for His

> Christ promises to bless His leaders in the mighty work of carrying out the Great Commission.

> Jesus wants His leaders to ask for His help. He will do what they ask in His name.

help. He will do what they ask in His name. His only condition is that God must get the glory for all that is accomplished.

Christ promised, *"If you ask anything in My name, I will do it"* (John 14:14). Therefore, the kingdom leader must have a strong prayer life. Regardless of the circumstances facing him, he hears Jesus' wonderful promise that He will do what the leader asks in His name.

If You Love Me, Obey Me

Jesus' disciples loved Him. They had been with Him from the beginning of His ministry and knew He loved them. He reminded them of the importance of loving Him. He said, *"If you love Me, keep My commandments"* (John 14:15).

The kingdom leader expresses his love for the Lord by obeying Him. Obeying the Lord may require great sacrifice. Still, Christ says to every generation of leaders, "If you love Me, obey Me."

I Am Always with You

These first kingdom leaders treasured Jesus' presence. What a thrill it had been to be close to such a wonderful person! Their lives had been changed by their association with Him. Now He was leaving them. Therefore, He said to them, *"I will not leave you orphans; I will come to you"* (John 14:18). Jesus promised to remain with these leaders through the presence of the Holy Spirit (John 14:16).

No leader can accomplish anything for God without the presence and power of the Holy Spirit. He is the Empowerer, the Helper, and the Interpreter of truth. The Holy Spirit will be with every kingdom leader in all circumstances. Jesus promises, *"Wherever I send you, whether to the remote mission field or to the church in the city, I will be with you always."* The kingdom leader is enabled and encouraged in his work because Jesus is always with him through the presence of the Holy Spirit.

The kingdom leader expresses his love for the Lord by obeying Him.

No leader can accomplish anything for God without the power and presence of the Holy Spirit.

I Will Give You My Peace

Jesus' relationship with the Father brought Him perfect peace. He conducted His work in the midst of grave danger with inner tranquility. He exhibited no irritation, frustration, fear, or turmoil in His life. He faced every adversity and opposition with serenity and peace of mind.

The first kingdom leaders faced many threats and dangers, but Jesus assured them that they did not have to be afraid. He promised them, *"Peace I leave with you, My peace I give to you; not as the world gives do I give to you. Let not your heart be troubled, neither let it be afraid" (John 14:27).*

Christ promises today's kingdom leaders His peace. Every kingdom leader needs that peace, peace that brings assurance and strength in the most difficult situations.

Abide in Me

Fruitfulness in leadership is not the result of training, location, or resources. It is the result of abiding in Christ. Jesus taught the first leaders this principle when He said, *"Every branch in Me that does not bear fruit He takes away; and every branch that bears fruit He prunes, that it may bear more fruit" (John 15:2).* As a branch must be in the vine to bear fruit, so must the fruit-bearing leader be in Christ.

Effectiveness in leadership is a result of abiding in Christ. He declared, *"I am the vine, you are the branches. He who abides in Me, and I in him, bears much fruit; for without Me you can do nothing" (John 15:5).* These words must have brought great joy and reassurance to those early leaders. They were not alone. They were part of Jesus, and they would bear much fruit.

Remember, I Love You

Jesus loved His disciples. He had chosen them, called them, and was sending them to do His work. He knew they were disturbed. He was leaving, and they wondered what would happen to

---

Christ promises today's kingdom leaders His peace, peace that brings assurance and strength in the most difficult situations.

Fruitfulness in leadership is not the result of training, location, or resources. It is the result of abiding in Christ.

Jesus chooses, calls, and loves His leaders.

them and to their relationship with Him. He assured them He would go on loving them. He said, *"As the Father loved Me, I also have loved you; abide in My love" (John 15:9).*

Every generation of kingdom leaders needs to know Jesus loves them. When they feel rejected by those they seek to serve, Jesus says, "Remember, I love you." He also reminds His leaders to abide in His love. He said, *"If you keep My commandments, you will abide in My love, just as I have kept My Father's commandments and abide in His love" (John 15:10).*

Remain Joyful

Joy should characterize the lives of kingdom leaders. Knowing that Jesus loved them and would never leave leave them brought gladness to the disciples' hearts. Jesus words to the disciples— *"These things I have spoken to you, that My joy may remain in you, and that your joy may be full" (John 15:11)*—are still valid for leaders today.

The joy Christ gives helps kingdom leaders overcome the trials and stresses of leadership. This joy comes to the kingdom leader who remains focused on God's Word and abides in Christ.

Love One Another

Jesus taught His disciples to love one another. He said to them, *"This is My commandment, that you love one another as I have loved you" (John 15:12).*

Believers, leaders especially, are to be known by their love for one another. Perhaps the saddest commentary on leaders is when competition, not love, controls and shapes their relationships. Jesus never intended for His leaders to compete with one another. He wants them to love one another and respect one another's calling from God.

You Are My Friends

Today, many leaders in the church feel alone and forsaken. They are discouraged, frustrated, afraid, and lonely. Leaders need friends, friends they can trust, friends in whom they can confide and with whom they can feel secure.

What better or greater friend could a kingdom leader have than the Lord Jesus Christ? Jesus assured His disciples that they were His friends. He said, *"No longer do I call you servants, for a servant does not know what his master is doing; but I have called you friends, for all things that I heard from My Father I have made known to you" (John 15:15).*

Kingdom leaders know Jesus considers them His trusted friends because He has confided in them what the Father has spoken to Him. The greatest assurance a kingdom leader can have that he is a friend of Jesus is to know what Jesus is doing in the world and to join Him.

I Have Chosen You

Jesus reminded His first leaders that He had chosen them to carry on His work. He said, *"You did not choose Me, but I chose you and appointed you that you should go and bear fruit, and that your fruit should remain, that whatever you ask the Father in My name He may give you" (John 15:16).*

The kingdom leader is chosen by the Lord Jesus to bear fruit. The fruit that results from the work Christ appointed him to do is timeless. It never decays, never withers. It is eternal. The kingdom leader must never forget that Jesus has chosen him and expects him to bear fruit .

Expect Opposition

The kingdom leader can expect persecution and trouble as he follows the leadership example set by Jesus Christ. Jesus' ministry is a vivid example of that reality. The Lord did not want His disciples to be surprised by the difficulties and opposition they would face. Therefore, He told then to *"remember the word that I said to you, 'A servant is not greater than his master.' If they persecuted Me, they will also persecute you. If they kept My word, they will keep yours also" (John 15:20).*

Kingdom leaders should not expect to be treated better than their Lord and Leader. They must remember that opposition comes to them because of people's unbelief and opposition to God. Did not Jesus say, *"But all these things they will do to you for My name's sake, because they do not know Him who sent Me" (John 15:21)*?

Listen to the Holy Spirit

Jesus provided the disciples everything they needed to be kingdom leaders. In preparing them for their work, He taught them the importance of relying on the Holy Spirit to carry out their leadership responsibilities. He promised kingdom leaders that the Holy Spirit would be their "Helper" (John 16:7).

The Holy Spirit convicts the world of sin. The leader's task is to speak the Word of God, not to convict of sin. As the leader declares the truth of Jesus Christ, the Spirit convicts the world of sin.

The Holy Spirit guides the leader in understanding the truth of God's Word (John 16:13). He teaches the leader the deep truths of God. Jesus said, *"All things that the Father has are Mine. Therefore I said that He will take of Mine and declare it to you" (John 16:15).* The Holy Spirit helps the leader understand where God is moving and what should be done by the church to join Him in His work.

Jesus' counsel to those first kingdom leaders is applicable for leaders in every culture and age. He gave to His disciples and has given to every kingdom leader since those days reassurance, encouragement, support, strength, and His presence.

Let His words, His presence, His everlasting promises find their place in your life, your heart, your calling, and your place of service. Let them be your joy, your peace, your confidence. They are your legacy, your heritage, your sacred trust.

The Holy Spirit helps the leader understand where God is moving and what should be done by the church to join Him in His work.

Let His words, His presence, and His everlasting promises find their place in your life, your heart, your calling, and your place of service. Let them be your joy, your peace, and your confidence. They are your legacy, your heritage, and your sacred trust.

98

Christ's Counsel for Kingdom Leaders

Do not be troubled.
I will come again.
I will bless your work.
I will do what you ask.
If you love Me, obey Me.
I am always with you.
I will give you my peace.
Abide in Me.
Remember, I love you.
Remain joyful.
Love one another.
You are my friends.
I have chosen you.
Expect opposition.
Listen to the Holy Spirit.

KINGDOM LEADER APPLICATION

TEACHING GUIDE

Overview

These teaching suggestions are designed to help church leaders study this book by analysis, synthesis, and evaluation. Interactive questions and group application activities are included. Teaching sessions will be enhanced if each participant has read the chapter being studied and has answered the reflective questions at the end of the chapter.

The leadership group should read and study this book together. The teaching suggestions can be used during weekly staff meeting, on annual retreats, or at a one-day leadership-enrichment conference.

You will need to photocopy and enlarge the graphics and line grids in this "Teaching Guide" in order to record your responses.

Teaching Suggestions:
Introduction
Interactive Questions

1. Use the following diagram to analyze the differences and similarities between the leadership style of secular business leaders and the leadership style of Christ-centered leaders. Fill in the empty spaces in the circles below with differences and similarities.

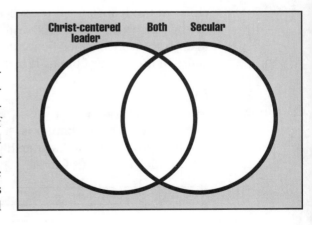

2. Define in your own words:
   A. The kingdom of God is _____
   _____
   _____.

   B. Jesus' position in the kingdom is _____
   _____
   _____.

3. Record the six kingdom principles that Jesus taught
(see pages 12–13).
   A _____
   B _____
   C _____
   D _____
   E _____
   F _____

4. Explain how understanding these principles can affect your
ministry in your church. _____
_____
_____
_____
_____
_____

Group Activity:
Divide the leadership group into teams. Assign the six kingdom principles to the teams. Each team is to decide how a basic understanding
of the assigned principle(s) will affect believers in its church. Each
team is to describe specific ministries that might start or continue because of the truth of the assigned principle(s).

Chapter One
Interactive Questions
1. The title of this chapter is "Jesus Christ: The Kingdom Leader."
Compare your personal leadership style to the kingdom leadership
style modeled by Jesus Christ. _____
_____
_____
_____
_____

2. The titles given to Jesus in the Scriptures describe His person, work, and leadership qualities. How does each of these descriptions influence your personal ministry and calling?

Jesus' Titles	Influence on My Ministry
A. KING OF KINGS	_____
B. LORD OF LORDS	_____
C. Captain of salvation	_____
D. Apostle	_____
E. High Priest	_____
F. Head of the body	_____
G. Chief Shepherd	_____
H. Overseer	_____
I. Preeminent One	_____

3. Review the fundamental kingdom leadership principles reflected in Jesus' titles.

A. Because Jesus is _____, kingdom leadership is _____.

B. Because Jesus is _____, kingdom leadership is _____.

C. Because Jesus is _____, kingdom leadership is _____.

D. Because Jesus is _____, kingdom leadership is _____.

E. Because Jesus is _____, kingdom leadership is _____.

F. Because Jesus is _____, kingdom leadership is _____.

G. Because Jesus is _____, kingdom leadership is _____.

H. Because Jesus is _____, kingdom leadership is _____.

I. Because Jesus is _____, kingdom leadership is _____.

4. Summarize in your own words kingdom leadership principle number 1._____
_____
_____
_____
_____

Group Activity

Discuss how you think your church would evaluate its leaders' practice of kingdom leadership as Jesus modeled it. Record your thoughts on a large sheet of newsprint. What are the strengths and weaknesses?

Chapter Two
Interactive Questions

1. Briefly explain the implications of the principle, "The call of God is the foundation for the church's work in the world," for your ministry and your church's ministry. _____
_____
_____
_____

2. According to Hebrews 3:2, Jesus "was faithful to the one who appointed Him."

A. Evaluate your faithfulness to your call to kingdom leadership.
_____
_____
_____
_____

B. How do you think your church would evaluate your faithfulness to kingdom leadership? _____
_____
_____
_____

C. What differences do you feel would exist in the two assessments? Why?_____
_____
_____

3. Reexamine the section, "Jesus Christ and His Response to the Call of God." Analyze to what degree...

A. You are totally submitted to the call of God. _____
_____
_____
_____

B. Your church is total submitted to the call of God. _____
_____
_____
_____

4. Summarize in your own words kingdom leadership principle number 2._____

_____

_____

_____

_____

Group Activity
Divide the leadership group into teams. Ask each team to study Jesus' call to one or more of the following: salvation, sanctification, security, service, and suffering. Ask each team to summarize the consequences when a church does *not* understand the particular call assigned to the team. Then the team should evaluate its church's specific understanding of that call.

Chapter Three
Interactive Questions
1. How do pressures forge your Christian character? _____

_____

_____

_____

_____

2. List a specific pressure that developed leadership character in your life? _____

_____

Are you experiencing a "forging" pressure now? _____
Identify it._____

3. "Too many church leaders mistakenly have spent all or most of their time developing preaching, administrative, and ministry skills without giving equal or greater attention to character building."
    A. Has this been true in your experience?_____
    B. How can a leader prioritize building Christlike character?

_____

_____

_____

4. Personalize the 13 essential character qualities of a leader as discussed on pages 39–43 and in 1 Timothy 3:1–7 by stating what you

intend to do to develop each particular character quality.
(Example: Verse 1-—I intend to begin immediately to renew and to
strengthen my desire to be the kingdom leader God called me to be.)

    A. Desire to serve
    B. Blameless
    C. Faithful spouse
    D. Temperate
    E. Sober-minded
    F. Hospitable
    G. Teacher
    H. No alcohol abuse
    I. Gentle
    J. Giver
    K. Family leader
    L. Mature
    M. Good reputation

5. Summarize in your own words kingdom leadership principle
number 3._____

_____

_____

_____

Group Activity

Jesus taught by using word pictures. Teach your church leaders by
placing these New Testament word pictures in the leaders' present-
day ministry situation. Divide the leaders into four teams named
teachers, soldiers, athletes, and farmers. Ask each team to act out a
skit that illustrates the characteristics of its assigned word-picture
group. (This can be done in discussion groups without actually enact-
ing a skit.)

Chapter Four
Interactive Questions

1. Satan tempted Jesus in what three categories? _____,
_____, and _____
Do you see Satan tempting God's ministers in these same categories
today? Why or why not?

_____

_____

_____

2. Jesus overcame Satan's temptations by using the _____.

3. Analyze your own temptations by listing them under each of these categories:

Needs	Ambition	Power
_____	_____	_____
_____	_____	_____
_____	_____	_____

4. List some Scriptures that will help you face such temptation.

_____   _____   _____

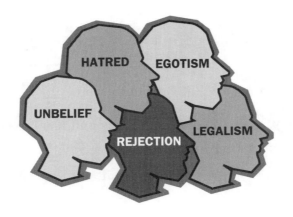

5. Jesus faced unbelief, hatred, rejection, egotism, and legalism. What kinds of opposition to spiritual truth do you see taking place today? _____

_____

6. Summarize in your own words kingdom leadership principle number 4._____

_____

_____

_____

Group Activity:
As church leaders, identify the strongholds in your ministry and church that are standing against God's work. Break into strategy teams and, using Jesus as your leadership model, develop a plan to deal with these strongholds.

Chapter Five
Interactive Questions

1. Kingdom vision is _____.

    A. Jesus expressed His vision of the mission of all believers in what Scripture? _____

    B. Write your own personal "marching orders" by paraphrasing these same verses. _____

    _____

2. How can a lack of kingdom vision deter a local church from accomplishing God's work? _____

    _____

3. Why is it vital for a kingdom leader to have a servant heart?

    _____

4. Do you feel you have a true servant's heart? _____

5. How can you develop or further develop this servant attitude?

    _____

6. What changes do you need to make in your leadership style to become a servant leader? _____

    _____

7. Using Christ as your leadership model, evaluate your leadership competencies as "weak, adequate, strong." Show how you are applying the competencies in your ministry.

Personal Competencies Evaluation

Competency	My Rating	How Applied in Ministry
Kingdom vision	_____	_____
Global vision	_____	_____
Servant heart	_____	_____
Leader builder	_____	_____
Communicator	_____	_____

Group Activity

To help the members of the church leadership group practice being kingdom leaders who utilize every believer's giftedness, ask them to prepare a large wall chart that shows how these ministry gifts are being or can be used in their churches.

Ministry Gifts	How Applied in Church Ministry
1. Administration	_____
2. Evangelism	_____
3. Exhortation	_____
4. Giving	_____
5. Helps	_____
6. Hospitality	_____
7. Leadership	_____
8. Mercy	_____
9. Prophecy	_____
10. Service	_____
11. Shepherding	_____
12. Teaching	_____

After completing the chart, design a plan to help church members discover their gifts and identify areas of ministry needing their gifts. [See "Kingdom Leadership Resources" for *Ministry Gifts Inventory Kit,* a valuable new resource for determining and applying each church member's ministry gifts.]

Chapter Six
Interactive Questions

1. Name the four essential functions that a kingdom leader must carry out: _____, _____, _____, _____.

2. Rate your present competency in each of these four essential functions as "excellent, good, fair, poor, very poor."

Function	My Rating
Leading	_____
Administering	_____
Ministering	_____
Communicating	_____

3. Complete these statements regarding your leadership skills:
   A. As a herald of God's message, I _____
   _____.

   B. As a teacher of Scripture, I _____
   _____.

   C. As a mentor to future leaders, I _____
   _____.

   D. As one who reproves and corrects, I _____
   _____.

4. Write the definition of a kingdom leader found on page 114.

_____

_____
_____
_____

5. In light of this definition, list additional leadership competencies you need to develop in your personal ministry._____

_____
_____

6. Summarize in your own words kingdom leadership principle number 6. _____

_____
_____
_____

Group Activity
Organize the church leadership group into teams to analyze your church's perception of its leaders' effectiveness in the essential functions of *leading, administering, ministering,* and *communicating.* Each team should assess leaders' strengths, weaknesses, opportunities for improvement, and obstacles to moving forward in these functions.

Chapter Seven
Interactive Questions
1. Each kingdom leader's path is personal and is designed by God. Reflect on when you became aware that God was calling you to be a kingdom leader. Write your understanding of what God has called you to do. _____

_____

2. Record the three leadership lessons learned from Jesus' example that are found on page 77.

    A. _____

    B. _____

    C. _____

3. Complete this leadership journey reflection. Answer the questions for each plateau you have passed through or are now on.

Leadership Journey Reflection
1. Beginning Leader
    A. What factors are you looking at to define your call from God?
    B. How has God gifted you to carry out His call?

C. What are you doing to insure that you focus on God's gift of leadership, not on your ability to develop leadership qualities?

D. What obstacles in your life are keeping you from developing as a kingdom leader ?

E. How are you preparing for the next leadership plateau?

2. Assimilating Leader

A. As you explore your leadership role, how well are you staying under God's authority?

B. What strengths have you discovered about your leadership abilities?

C. What are crises and troubles teaching you about leadership?

D. What ways have you found to relate to other kingdom leaders?

E. What are you doing to build relationships in your church?

F. How are you preparing for the next leadership plateau?

3. Building Leader

A. What is your overall leadership strategy?

B. How are you using your leadership influence to develop kingdom workers in your church?

C. What is your response to how well the church is embracing your leadership?

D. How are you guarding against complacency when things are going well?

E. How are you responding to the trials of leadership?

F. How are you preparing for the next plateau?

4. Achieving Leader

A. In the midst of human recognition, how are you guarding against forgetting that your call is from God?

B. In what ways are you helping to develop emerging kingdom leaders?

C. Name some leadership principles you are sharing with the new generation of leaders?

D. Whom are you identifying as potential ministry leaders?

E. What are you doing to prepare for the next plateau?

5. Maturing Leader

A. What is the focus of your ministry?

B. In what ways have you responded appropriately to ordeals in leadership?

C. How are you multiplying your efforts through others?

D. Name the beginning, assimilating, and building leaders with whom you are sharing?

E. What obstacles in your life are preventing you from moving to the next plateau? How do you plan to deal with them?

6. Refocusing Leader

A. In what direction is God leading you now?

B. How are you remaining focused on the work God has called you to do? Are you completing that work with a strong finish?

C. If you were at the beginning leader plateau again, what would you do differently?

Group Activity

Divide the church leaders into teams and assign each team to a leadership plateau. Ask each team to...

1. List the characteristics of its assigned plateau.

2. Answer these questions:

A. What are the strengths of the leader at this plateau?

B. What questions is this kingdom leader asking?

C. What obstacles can stand in the way of leadership growth at this stage?

D. How does the kingdom leader prepare for the next stage?

Chapter Eight

Interactive Question

Ask each participant to read the counsel Jesus gave kingdom leaders. Ask yourself, Is this counsel *convicting, encouraging, challenging?* Explain your reasoning. Record your answers.

1. "Do not be troubled."_____

2. "I will come again."_____

3. "I will bless your work."_____

4. "I will do what you ask."_____

5. "If you love Me, obey Me." _____

6. "I am always with you."_____

7. "I will give you my peace." _____

8. "Abide in Me." _____

9. "Remember, I love you." _____

10. "Remain joyful." _____

11. "Love one another." _____

12. "You are my friends." _____

13. "I have chosen you." ————————————————————

14. "Expect opposition." ————————————————————

15. "Listen to the Holy Spirit." ————————————————

How do Jesus' words affect your call? Which situation(s) in your ministry do these words touch?

Group Activity

Ask each member of the leadership group to select one of Jesus' counsels that is ministering especially to him or her at that moment. Ask the members to share the selections and explain why they are ministering to them at that particular time.

Close with a time of praise and thanksgiving for being called as kingdom leaders.

KINGDOM LEADERSHIP RESOURCES

The Empowered Leader: Ten Keys to Servant Leadership by Calvin Miller (Nashville: Broadman & Holman Publishers, 1995) explores the call to servant leadership and offers 10 keys to the kind of leadership God desires, using King David as a model and a source of precepts for servant leadership today.

Growing Churches (Item # 1506), a quarterly journal, reports the latest, most significant developments in church growth. Each issue features interviews with church growth leaders, examples and models drawn from many denominations, national statistics, practical resources for traditional and innovative worship services, a Reader Forum accessible by FAX, mail or SBCNet, and biblical studies on spiritual leadership.

Jesus on Leadership: Developing Servant Leaders Kit by Gene Wilkes (Nashville: Lifeway Press, 1996; Item # 7700-71) equips the potential, the new, and the experienced leader to serve effectively on the church ministry team and to develop other leaders. *Jesus on Leadership* includes a 90-minute videotape, a 60-minute audiocassette, a computer diskette, a facilitator's guide, and one copy of the workbook.

Kingdom Principles for Church Growth by Gene Mims (Nashville: Convention Press, 1994; Item # 5120-20) presents and explains the "1•5•4 Principle"—based on the Great Commission—that leads to balanced church growth through effective leadership.

115

Kingdom Principles Growth Strategies by Gene Mims and Mike Miller (Nashville: Convention Press, 1995; Item # 5600-04) contains an instruction guide, a copy of *Kingdom Principles for Church Growth,* a leader's guide, two videos, a video viewing guide, a *Ministry Gifts Inventory,* thirteen overhead transparencies and a strategic events calendar. *Kingdom Principles Growth Strategies* is intended to assist church leaders in implementing the growth strategies inherent in the Great Commission and the kingdom of God.

Ministry Gifts Inventory (Nashville: Convention Press, 1996; Item # 5600-38) is a 12-page resource to assist individual church members in identifying and understanding their ministry gifts.

Ministry Gifts Inventory Software Kit (Nashville: Convention Press, 1996; Item # 5621-55) is designed to help a church keep track of the ministry gifts of individual members. The kit includes two 3.5 inch diskettes (formatted for Microsoft Windows 3.1 or higher), user-friendly installation instructions, and 25 copies of *Ministry Gifts Inventory.*